sex is...

HOW *strong* MARRIAGES CULTIVATE *stronger* CHURCHES

Kevin J. Moore, PhD

Carpenter's Son Publishing

Sex Is… How Strong Marriages Cultivate Stronger Churches

Published by Carpenter's Son Publishing, Franklin, Tennessee

Published in association with Larry Carpenter of Christian Book Services, LLC
www.christianbookservices.com

Cover and Interior Layout Design by Suzanne Lawing

Edited by Gail Fallen

Printed in the United States of America

978-1-946889-89-8

Dedicated to Stephanie,
the love of my life.

I also want to express my gratitude
to those whose testimonies appear in this book.
Thank you for encouraging others by telling your stories.

WHAT PEOPLE ARE SAYING ABOUT *SEX IS . . .*

"My pastor Kevin Moore has offered to all of us an outstanding statement and helpful analysis of one of those seemingly "untouchable" subjects. His treatment of this topic, SEX, which literally touches all of us as creations of our loving heavenly Father, provides us with a unique tool. In a tasteful and direct manner Dr. Moore expresses truth from Song of Solomon that should be required reading for every man, woman, pastor, counselor, married couple, engaged couple, and single person. My wife of forty-eight years and I have read and discussed the book. Because of it our marriage will be even better, and that is saying a lot . . . believe me."

Dr. Edwin Jenkins
Retired/Redirected Pastor and Denominational Missionary
Huntsville, AL

"I wish there had been such a manual on intimacy when my husband and I married forty-seven years ago. Good to know God's Word always gets it right!"

Susan Keyes
Bible Study Leader, Park Cities Presbyterian Church
Dallas, TX

"The manner in which the book tied together how strong marriages help build strong, effective churches helped us realize the degree of fulfillment we have in our marriage affects not only our family but also our interactions at church and in the community. The true stories that were woven throughout the book helped reinforce the points being made. We are now definitely more aware that God designed us to thrive in our marriages so that He is glorified at home and church."

Trish Morris
Executive Director, Huntsville Pregnancy Resource Center
Huntsville, AL

"After reading this book I was overwhelmed with the fact that healthy marriages lay the foundation for healthy families, which leads to healthy churches. Thus, it is in the best interest of both couples and churches to work diligently at strengthening marriages. Dr. Moore, with his practical "how to" teaching and insights derived from God's Holy Word, zeroes in on how couples can enhance their sexual intimacy and strengthen their marriages. A great book for couples to read and discuss together."

Dr. Charlie Howell
Executive Director of Missions, Madison Baptist Association
Huntsville, AL

"*Sex Is.* . . . The title of the book stopped me short. And yet, in a culture in which sex is cheapened to brief hook-ups and enticing screen images, Dr. Kevin Moore's book presents a beautiful picture of what God intended His design for covenant marriage to be, with sexual intimacy taking a central place in a committed relationship between husband and wife. Song of Solomon is the springboard for practical discussions of how to include pursuit, love, and friendship in the marriage union in such a way that sexual intimacy is the fulfillment of the union. Kevin describes marital intimacy as a wonderful feast and leads the reader gently through a minefield of objections and obstacles to arrive at the unity that God intended in His marriage creation. After fifty-one years in a wonderful committed marriage, I found encouragement, refreshment, and renewal in Kevin's book. I pray that this book will be used to bring life and joy and deepened intimacy in many marriages and that God will be deeply glorified."

Jane Pope
Former Teaching Leader, Bible Study Fellowship International
Abilene, TX, and Nairobi, Kenya
US Director, Faith House Ministries of Africa, Inc.

"STOP THE ALLEGORY! The truth of Song of Solomon is far too important to leave in the hands of allegory. In celebration of God's good gift of sex, Kevin Moore presents biblical truth for a generation in desperate need of pure and passionate sexuality."

Dr. Michael Feese
Senior Pastor, Mount Zion Baptist Church
Alvord, TX

"Refreshing! The efforts of the culture to hijack the true meaning of intimacy has been astounding. Dr. Moore recaptures the beauty of the intimacy between husband and wife as it is truly meant to be. This exposition of Song of Solomon is a masterful work portraying the uniqueness of the gospel through the blessings of marriage."

Casey Johnson
President of Exit 416 Ministries
Bastrop, LA

"Kevin Moore gives both a great exposition of Song of Solomon and practical applications of these inspired truths to one of the truly elusive components of human relationships: sex. *Sex Is…* will help believers love marital sex the way God designed them to love it. This book was insightful and practical—a real blessing to the church."

Dr. Kevin Jordan
Senior Pastor, Cana Baptist Church
Burleson, TX

"A song is always of interest to a church musician. This ancient song captures the interest and imagination of any person who desires to have a wonderful union with their life choice of a God-given marriage partner. With keen insights from Dr. Moore, the analysis and focus of both the Christian marriage and its importance to itself and the life of the church are made extremely clear in this easy-to-read book. Anyone who reads it will have no doubts as to God's intended purpose for marriage. The book will help you fall in love all over again with your spouse as you read about God's intended purposes for your unique bond of love."

MARK BLANKENSHIP
Youth and Adult Music Editor for LifeWay, Retired
Huntsville, AL

"In our culture of sexual confusion, God's good gift of sex has been perverted, stealing from married couples the powerful intimacy that makes for strong marriages. In his book *Sex Is . . .* my friend Kevin Moore lays out a scriptural prescription for what ails many marriages today . . . a lack of authentic sexual intimacy. You'll find Kevin's book profoundly biblical (based on Song of Solomon), emotionally engaging, and thoroughly practical. It's also a great resource for churches to use in equipping believers for healthy marriages."

DR. MICHAEL D. DEAN
Senior Pastor, Travis Avenue Baptist Church
Fort Worth, TX

"Kevin Moore's latest book, *Sex Is . . . How Strong Marriages Cultivate Stronger Churches,* is a much-needed addition to the bookshelf of any Christian seeking to strengthen his/her marriage. The biblical insights, practical applications, and inspiring testimonies make this book an encouraging tool in the hands of married couples regardless of how many (or few) years they have been married. Dr. Moore's book is highly recommended—not only for premarital counseling but also for the biblical counseling of any couple seeking wisdom and help with this largely neglected topic."

SCOTT BRYANT
Worship Pastor, Lamar Baptist Church
Arlington, TX

"In an increasingly confusing and changing culture regarding sex and sexuality, we desperately need to hear from God—the Creator and Designer of sex—and He is not silent! Kevin Moore has given us a much-needed corrective in a biblical and practical look at the celebration of the sexuality that God always intended for our joy. Don't just read it, but let the Word of God enrich your marriage and strengthen the church as you put it into practice to the glory of God."

MICHAEL CARTER
Senior Pastor, First Baptist Church of Guymon
Guymon, OK

"Dr. Moore's book *Sex Is. . .* is one that has been needed in the church for a long time. We are constantly being bombarded with Satan's lies. These lies are the most pervasive in the area of sexual intimacy. These lies are in our music, movies, and advertisements. The church has been focused more on what not to do in the area of sex rather than what to do. Dr. Moore's book is a very practical, Scripture-based guide toward what to do in order to create healthy relationships and healthy marriages. Its application is universal. It is as relevant to those contemplating marriage as well as to those who have enjoyed fifty years of marital bliss. *Sex Is. . .* is a must read for all those wanting to achieve a healthy marriage and healthy relationship!"

BRENT COOPER
Board Chairman, Southeast Asia Ministries
Dallas, TX

"Sex: the topic where Christians are quiet and the culture is L O U D. It's time to start asking, 'Is my understanding of sex based upon what the Bible actually says, or did I come to my conclusions from Hollywood, various authors, and the media?' Culture is giving you its opinion. Now it's time to hear God's opinion on sex. John 10:10 sums it all up. When we accept God's way we experience life. When we reject God's way we experience destruction. Let's embrace the path that leads to life. In Dr. Moore's book, *Sex Is . . .* you will see what God has to say about sex. I recommend this book for anyone who has ever thought about sex."

TIM MILNER
Lead Pastor, Essential Church,
Huntsville, AL

"Song of Solomon is all about God's good gift of sexual intimacy in marriage, and this book aims to show why sex is such a good gift of God. *Sex Is . . .* serves as a tool for married couples to grow in intimacy because it is designed to be read through, prayed through, and discussed together. It is biblical, practical, and accessible. The testimonies scattered throughout the book from couples with various life issues at various stages of marriage are hope-filled and realistic. The author's positive portrayal of sex combined with the section on helpful advice for those struggling sexually are worth the price of the book! Finally, this book consistently and uniquely demonstrates the connection between a healthy sex life in marriage, healthy marriages, and healthy churches. May those who read this book seek by faith to embrace God's design for sexual intimacy in marriage for the glory of Christ and the health of Christian marriages and churches."

Dallas Vandiver
Spiritual Life Coordinator, Christian Academy of Louisville
Louisville, KY

"Children of God who yearn to know and interact with the Lord's thoughts on sex will be extremely blessed by Dr. Kevin Moore's simple, yet fascinating, look at what the Bible offers in Song of Solomon. It is works like *Sex Is . . .* that remind us of the sufficiency of Scripture in all aspects of our lives, including sexual intimacy."

Jerry Horine
Senior Pastor, Friendship Baptist Church
Montalba, TX

Contents

Introduction

STRONG MARRIAGES, STRONG FAMILIES, STRONG CHURCHES

You are about to plunge into the ocean depths of marital delight! God, who is infinitely loving, has given you and your spouse a precious gift that He wants you to enjoy to the fullest. As you learn to love your spouse magnificently in the bedroom, God will nourish your marriage in marvelous ways. If you are willing and ready to improve your love life, get ready for an avalanche of delight. From sheer physical satisfaction to an unbreakable unity, God has so many blessings waiting for you as you learn how to feast on each other! God loves marriages and He wants yours to be a success. The King of the Universe wants to help you to succeed in your marriage. God wants to use the strength and joy of your marriage to impact your family and your church.

Why Did God Devote a Book of the Bible to Sex?

With other pressing issues such as the depravity of humanity and the impending judgment of the world, why devote such attention to what goes on in the privacy of a marriage? Why does a book that does not even mention God's name get included in the Bible? If you have ever pondered these questions, you are not alone. Maybe you have waded into the colorful imagery and found yourself puzzled by the archaic metaphors, or perhaps you have avoided the book altogether. In general, I don't think most people know what to do with Song of Solomon.

Why should we pay attention to Song of Solomon? Song of Solomon is the inspired Word of God. For this reason alone, Song of Solomon demands our attention. According to 2 Timothy 3:16–17, "All Scripture is God-breathed and is useful for teaching, rebuking, correcting and training in righteousness, so that the servant of God may be thoroughly equipped for every good work." Song of Solomon is inspired in the very same way that the Gospel of John is inspired. It is just as inspired as the apostle Paul's letters in the New Testament. The church needs Song of Solomon just as it needs the book of Proverbs. There are no levels of inspiration. Something is either God-breathed, or it is not. Song of Solomon is God-breathed!

Based upon the promise of 2 Timothy 3:16, we can safely conclude that Song of Solomon is useful for teaching, rebuking, correcting, and training in righteousness. In other words, the Body of Christ needs teaching and correcting in the area of sexual intimacy. Notice it's not just that marriages need Song of Solomon, the church needs it! The church needs training in righteousness as it pertains to the covenant of marriage. None of us wants to be spiritually immature when it comes to the issue of sexual intimacy. God has given you a book that is incredibly "useful," and it is right at your fingertips. Why miss out on the incredible opportunity to learn about sex from the One who created it?

The purpose for studying something useful for teaching, rebuking, correcting, and training in righteousness is so that we might be "thoroughly equipped for every good work" (2 Tim. 3:17). If we don't study Song of Solomon, we will miss out on something that God intended to prepare us for work in His kingdom. There is always a kingdom aspect to God's Word. As you study Song of Solomon, God will make you more useful for service in His kingdom. To be more specific, here are three areas in your life that will benefit greatly.

Strong Marriages

God wants to strengthen your marriage. Marriages in the church are hurting. Not only is the divorce rate far too high among Christians, but marriages that do last are not always healthy. A healthy sex life promotes strong marriages. Certainly other factors also cultivate strong marriages, but not to the exclusion of a healthy sex life.[1] Christians sitting in the pews have questions about sexual intimacy but don't always know where to find answers. Where does a Christian man or woman go when they experience problems in their sex life? How can they feel comfortable talking about something that the church has largely ignored? Sexual intimacy fortifies marriages against temptation. It serves like a gravitational force that drives you relentlessly to your spouse. It cultivates an abundance of joy in a relationship like nothing else. Intimacy strengthens a marriage against constant satanic assault. When couples experience problems with sexual intimacy, their relationship suffers. When marriages suffer, the unavoidable conclusion is that entire families suffer.

Strong Families

Families flourish when we love our spouse well. Every relationship in the home is positively impacted when a husband and wife love each other magnificently. One of the greatest gifts you can give to your children is the example of a godly marriage. They need to know what it looks like for a husband and wife to be deeply in love. The example of a godly marriage will impact them far more than whatever money you leave them in your will. When difficulties arise in their own marriages, they need to be able to look back on how their parents loved each other. The example of a godly marriage will serve as a glorious pattern for them to emulate. The goal in marriage is never to tolerate each other, but to experience the joy of loving each other.

---

1. This discussion, along with the remainder of the book, presumes the physical health of both partners that would allow for sexual intimacy.

Will your children remember your deep, abiding love for your spouse? Will they remember the affection and devotion you had for each other? Or will they remember how often the two of you fought? No relationship is perfect, but you want your children to have a living, breathing example of what an awesome marriage looks like. They will never see this in your marriage if you are constantly at odds over the issue of sex. Worse, they may repeat your same patterns of behavior in their own marriage. Entire generations will be affected by how you love your spouse. And churches are filled with far too many examples of unhappy marriages. Children from Christian homes should not have to grow up in an environment filled with dissension. When families suffer under the tyranny of unhealthy marriages, entire churches suffer!

Strong Churches

Your sex life is not ultimately about your personal gratification. God has a missional purpose in your marriage that extends far beyond you. Strong marriages contribute to strong families, which, in turn, cultivate stronger churches. Is it really so strange to see a connection between a marriage and the health of God's people? The community of faith punctuates Song of Solomon with celebration over the love that these two share together.

> We rejoice and delight in you; we will praise your love more than wine. How right they are to adore you! (1:4)
>
> Eat, friends, and drink; drink your fill of love. (5:1)

The believing community in Song of Solomon has an acute awareness of how important and significant a loving marriage is. We cannot separate the concept of marriage from the community of faith.

How can a church have a strong witness for Jesus when many of its families are privately hurting in dysfunctional marriages? Is it even possible to cultivate a spirit of love and unity in a church when there are so many unhappy families? No degree of excellence in ministry can compensate for the pain that families experience. And perhaps the decline in churches is not always a symptom of ineffective programing or leadership. Some churches are unhealthy because they are comprised of unhealthy families. Unhealthy families cripple the effectiveness of churches. This is more or less how pollution works as well. We have laws against dumping toxic waste into rivers because of the devastation that it causes downstream. It doesn't matter how far upstream you go; the pollution will eventually wreak havoc on everything below. The scope of the damage might shock those who thought the pollution would be mostly confined. In the same way, what goes on in the privacy of a marriage will eventually affect the body of Christ. Love between a husband and wife will benefit the church in wonderful ways. Bitterness and dissension will also trickle down and impact the church. This means that we need to talk about sex.

Let's Talk about Sex

Why on earth would we be silent when God has said so much about sex?[2] He's not embarrassed by the subject, nor does He want His children to be. He addresses sex over and over in Scripture and even devotes an entire book of the Bible to the subject. Song of Solomon is not a shy or muted explanation of sexual intimacy. Nothing about Song of Solomon is bashful or timid. The author is not stumbling awkwardly through the subject as though he had something to be ashamed of. Song of Solomon is a lively and animated celebration of God's wonderful gift. These lovers are positively triumphant about their love for each other. So much so, they sing of their love.

Also called the Song of Songs, Song of Solomon represents the greatest love song ever written.[3] There is no shortage of love songs in

---

2. The following are just a few of those passages: Gen. 4:1, 17, 25; 19:5, 33–35; 29:23; 34; Exod. 22:19; Lev. 18:6–30; 20:15–19; Num. 25:1–8; Deut. 23:18; 27:21; 16:1; 19:22; 2 Sam. 16:22; Prov. 5:19; 6:26; 7:9–27; 23:27; Song of Sol.; Matt. 15:19; Mark 7:21; Rom. 1:24, 26–27; 13:13; 1 Cor. 5:1; 6:13–20; 10:8; 2 Cor. 12:21; Gal. 5:19; Eph. 5:3; 1 Thess. 4:3; Jude 1:7; Rev. 2:14, 20; 9:21.
3. In Hebrew, the title of the book is literally "Song of Songs" or "The Greatest Song."

our world. But how many of these songs depict the kind of love we see in Song of Solomon? Many love songs today represent a whimsical love that is driven only by selfishness, alcohol, and poor decisions. Songs that celebrate one night stands are hardly worthy of their beautiful melodies. But the powerful love represented in Song of Solomon is worthy of the most sonorous jubilation. Love that endures and overcomes deserves a song like this one.

Even the community of faith is jubilant about the love that these two have for each other. Their friends and family are not rolling their eyes and saying, "Get over it already." They aren't looking condescendingly at this young couple knowing that their love will eventually fade. They aren't telling them, "Shh, be quiet." Instead, the community applauds their passionate desire for each other, saying, "We rejoice and delight in you; we will praise your love more than wine"(1:4). Song of Solomon is not just a celebration of sex but also a celebration of sexual intimacy within the covenant of marriage.

Our world has, in many ways, lost sight of the beauty of marriage. More and more people are choosing to cohabitate without any desire to enter the covenant of marriage. According to one Barna study, only one-third of Gen Xers and Millennials believe that sexual intimacy should unite a man and woman in marriage.[4] For many Millennials, sex is about "self-expression and personal fulfillment" and less about intimacy or marriage.[5] Symptomatic of these trends of thought is the fact that fewer and fewer people are getting married. Is marriage between a man and a woman becoming a new alternative lifestyle? According to the Pew Research Center, 72 percent of adults in America were married in 1960, compared to only 52 percent in 2008.[6] There has never been a greater need to study Song of Solomon.

---

4. Barna Group, "What Americans Believe about Sex, January 14, 2016, https://www.barna.com/research/what-americans-believe-about-sex/.
5. Ibid.
6. Pew Research Center, "The Decline of Marriage and the Rise of New Families," November 18, 2010, http://www.pewsocialtrends.org/2010/11/18/ii-overview/.

There is nothing about marriage that hinders sexual intimacy. To the contrary, we see that the loving boundary of marriage provides the optimal arena for the sexual relationship to flourish far beyond what most people think is even possible. God, who created sexual intimacy, knows exactly how it should be enjoyed. So why doesn't the church talk more about sex?

A Silent Church

When was the last time you heard a sermon series through Song of Solomon? I'm not talking about railing against sexual sin but a systematic treatment of healthy sexuality in marriage. I'm guessing that you haven't. In fact, after growing up in the church, I cannot recall even one of my pastors giving a systematic treatment to the issue. Personally, I was very hesitant for years to teach through Song of Solomon. Have you ever studied sexual intimacy in a Sunday school or a discipleship class? My guess is that unless you listened to a podcast or went to a special marriage conference, you have not heard much said about sexual intimacy.

Do you know when the subject is routinely raised? In marriage counseling sessions, when division over this subject has reached a feverish pitch. Silence on the subject of sexual intimacy in churches has not fared well. Will we hide behind an overzealous and misplaced sense of propriety while marriages suffer? Only a false piety ignores the issue of sexual intimacy, given the amount of attention that God devotes to the subject in the Bible. Let's not allow our sense of propriety to keep us from growing and learning in the area of sexual intimacy.

While the church has treated the subject of sex as largely taboo, the secular world cannot stop talking about it. Mo Isom captures this sad state of affairs:

> While society twists, perverts, cheapens, and idolizes it, we—the church—are relatively silent about it. Awkwardly stumbling around it. Running from it. Building desperate rule lists of dos and don'ts. And as a result allowing the sanctity of God to be

stolen by the insatiable lust of the lost. Somewhere along the way we've allowed ourselves to be drowned out of the conversation.[7]

When it comes to the issues of sexuality, our society has taken the place of vacuous pulpits with errant messages. Our culture is obsessed with sex. Through movies, music, and games, generations of people have been have mesmerized with lies about sex. Sex, to many people, is just the narcissistic pursuit of pleasure. Our culture embraces sexual expression without any regard for what the Bible teaches. Our society champions nearly every form of sexual gratification while simultaneously ignoring the painful consequences of sin. All the while, God's design of marriage is mocked as antiquated and irrelevant. When it comes to sex, secular society is fascinated with something they are so thoroughly confused about. Countless thousands of destroyed lives testify to this complete confusion. There is somebody, however, who knows all about sexual intimacy—someone we should be learning from: God.

Why would you ask God about something that seems so secular in nature? The answer is simple: God created sexual intimacy. Sex was God's idea. It is not the triumph of human ingenuity or creative expression. It is not the byproduct of a Darwinian process by which humanity desperately tries to avoid extinction. No, sex is the gift of God. God created humanity with sexual compatibility and commanded them to be fruitful and fill the earth (Gen. 1:27–28). Sex is a premier example of the James 1:17 principle; everything God gives is "good and perfect." God loves you so much that He chose to populate the earth through intense acts of pleasure. God is good!

Since God created sex, there is no reason to think of it as unspiritual or secular. God created sex and knows exactly how we should enjoy it. The topic of sex does not need to be taboo in the church; instead, it needs to be taught. Churches must go far beyond the message that

---

7. Mo Isom, *Sex, Jesus and the Conversations the Church Forgot* (Grand Rapids: Baker Books, 2018), 12.

"Sex before marriage is wrong!" What about sex after you get married? Unfortunately, not much is said about sex after marriage. Through our reticence we might unintentionally be sending the message that there is not much to learn about sex after marriage. Having sex is not the quintessential arrival point of your sexuality. Not even close. We need to learn and grow in the area of sexual intimacy just as we need to grow in other areas of our spiritual life.

The church should be talking about sex every bit as much as God talks about it in the Bible. As we study God's Word, we will discover just how wonderful the gift of sex is. Those sitting in the pews need to understand how glorious it can be when it is enjoyed within the covenant of marriage. The Word of God also exposes the lies of the Enemy where sex is concerned. The Bible "unmasks the one-night stands . . . the culture-crazed hookups and the promiscuity carried out in the darkness for what they really are—primitive, self-serving, impatient splurges that cheapen the value of the gift we've been given."[8] Young people need to grasp just how incredible sex can be if they do things God's way. Perish the thought that young people develop their understanding of human sexuality from their peers or through popular culture. Even those who have been married for many years need to grow in their understanding of how to minister to their spouse sexually. Every Christian should understand how sexual intimacy can strengthen their marriage so that they can be more effective in their service to Christ. The church cannot be silent about sex. If we are, our silence will serve as a tacit endorsement of all the perversion in our culture. Such reticence will also allow those struggling in their marriage to languish in despair without answers to their pressing questions.

For the church, the cost for reticence on the issue of sexual intimacy is too high. Christians need to learn how to leverage this precious gift to glorify the God who gave it. That's right, sexual activity

---

8. Ibid., 169.

can be *incredibly* glorifying to Christ as we enjoy it in the manner prescribed in the Bible. If we don't acknowledge the Godward purpose of sexual intimacy, we cannot enjoy the best of what God intended. I like the Godward emphasis that Paul Tripp sees in the gift of pleasure: "Pleasure exists to put God in my face and remind me that I was made by him and for him."[9] There is no possibility of enjoying sexual intimacy to its fullest while ignoring the God who created it.

The church must also speak out about sexual intimacy because people are suffering grievously underneath the tyranny of their sinful choices. It is not possible to overstate the incredible suffering that so many have experienced because of sin. Millions of people have devastated their lives and the lives of those they love the most through their sexual sin. Nearly everybody reading this book has felt the sting of sexual sin. Unspeakable shame and guilt follow these sinful choices, rendering all of us desperate for the message of grace. The church must speak.

Interpretation of Song of Solomon

A brief word about the interpretation of Song of Solomon is in order, since it is one of the most misunderstood books in the Bible. Historically, an allegorical interpretation of Song of Solomon has been favored. A number of the church fathers and theologians through the ages have preferred to interpret the book as an allegory of Christ's love for the church. While no orthodox theologian would question Christ's love for the church, there is not sufficient evidence within Song of Solomon that the reader should interpret the book in such a nonliteral manner.[10] Song of Solomon is best interpreted as a collection of love songs written by Solomon. Song of Solomon is a jubilant celebration of sexual intimacy between a husband and wife who are totally committed to each other. Song of Solomon exalts sex as the physical expression of a powerful love in a godly marriage.

---

9. Paul David Tripp, *Sex in a Broken World: How Christ Redeems What Sin Distorts* (Wheaton, IL: Crossway, 2018), 73.

What Kind of Book Is This?

More than anything, *Sex Is . . .* endeavors to be truthful. It's time to speak the truth about sexual intimacy. In the pages of this book, you may encounter some things that you don't want to hear. All of the major principles in this book are taken directly from God's Word. *Sex Is . . .* explores the foundational principles from Song of Solomon that will help you cultivate a biblical understanding of sexual intimacy. In these pages, you will discover what God accomplishes in your marriage as you love your spouse well. If God says it, the church should teach it. The church must speak with clarity and conviction because God has spoken so clearly about sex in His Word.

Second, this book is practical. This is not a philosophical treatment of the issue of sexual intimacy. Instead, *Sex Is . . .* contains practical advice that you can put to work in your marriage today. You will explore why marriage is the ideal paradigm for experiencing a wonderful sex life. You will learn about the kinds of things that add fuel to the fires of intimacy in your marriage. You will also learn about the things that are sure to extinguish your passion. We will also tackle some important questions such as "What do I do if my spouse is not as interested in sex?" or "If sex is so unifying, why do we fight so much about it?" or "How does God want me to pursue my spouse?"

---

10. One of the more imaginative interpretations of Song of Solomon has been by those who propose that the book lays out a paradigm for the proper progression of a relationship. The primary divisions proposed by some would be friendship, dating, and courtship, then the ensuing intimacy within the covenant of marriage. The primary problem with this interpretation is the overtly sexual imagery throughout the book. Those who maintain mere friendship in chapter 1 must explain away why she beckons him to bring her into his bedroom in the fourth verse of the book. Another vexing question would be why the woman describes the man as "resting between her breasts." Chapter 2 ends with her talking about him browsing among the lilies. Surely, we would not want this language to characterize friendship or courtship between a man and a woman. It might be presumptuous to impose Western ideals like dating on top of a poetic book written centuries before Christ. By design, Hebrew poetry is terse. Such brevity does not easily allow for the explanation of these stages or the chronological development of the stages in a godly relationship. Certainly, the burden of proof would rest on the side of those who propose this interpretation of the Song of Solomon.

This book contains real testimonies from people just like you who have struggled in their marriages. Some have been married for a short time and others for many years. Their stories will encourage and inspire you to do marriage God's way. Their pain is real, but so are their victories.

Every marriage is unique. The descriptions of how husbands and wives sometimes struggle may not always be representative of your marriage. In certain respects, your marriage will be very different from the tendencies portrayed in this book. It is not possible to address all of the idiosyncrasies of every marriage. If this book addresses a common problem that you don't experience in your marriage, praise the Lord. Be thankful that the Lord has already taught you how to navigate around the common pitfall. On the other hand, you may be experiencing an issue not addressed in this book. In that case, I would encourage you to allow the discussions in the book to provide a starting point to working through your specific challenge. Ask the Lord to show you how the principles from Song of Solomon can help you in your situation. You might also want to seek out another couple to mentor you through the challenges in your marriage. If your marriage is experiencing significant problems beyond the scope of this book, I encourage you to seek out a Christian counselor to guide you through the hardship(s) you are experiencing.

Along the way you may encounter a few things that you wish you had done differently through the years of marriage. Even in the writing of this book, I encountered my own faults and flaws—not once, but over and over. None of us is perfect. Neither you nor your spouse has done everything just right in your marriage. The point of this book is not to make you wallow in regret, but to encourage you toward the greatest intimacy in your marriage. Let's look forward, not backward. There is plenty of time to enjoy the best of what God intended sexual intimacy to be in your marriage.

Finally, this book is respectful of both men and women. God knew exactly what He was doing when He created men and women differently. We live in a world that has a difficult time acknowledging the beauty of God's design. Our society has created a toxic environment where aspects of masculinity and femininity are mocked and maligned. God's Word gives dignity to men and women. Disrespectful words and actions based purely upon one's gender must be rejected as evil and antithetical to the gospel. The differences between a man and a woman accomplish a wonderful compatibility within a marriage where both partners are seeking a closer relationship with Jesus. This book acknowledges the beauty of God's design and encourages husbands and wives to love each other magnificently!

Is This Book for Me?

Every married couple can benefit from learning more about what God has to say about sexual intimacy. Are you ready to experience a more fulfilling sexual relationship with your spouse? Do you find that you are not on the same page when it comes to sex? Has the subject of sex been a source of contention in your marriage? Are you ready to improve your sex life, but just don't know where to start? Have you struggled to understand what Song of Solomon means for your sex life? If you have answered yes to any of these questions, you will benefit greatly from *Sex Is. . . .* If, on the other hand, you are quite content and not even the least bit curious to see if there could be more to sexual intimacy, please set this book down right now. But maybe the question is not so much about whether you are satisfied. The question you need to be asking is, "Is my spouse satisfied?" Because if your spouse is not completely satisfied, then maybe you are not finished growing in this area. I don't think we ever arrive at the place where we no longer need to learn how to love our spouse. The most significant issue, however, is whether your marriage is in a place where you can be a blessing to your believing community and a hurting world.

Whether you are newly married or have been married for many years, this book is for you. God's truth regarding sexual intimacy is always relevant, regardless of what stage of life you are in. For those of you who are newly married, this book will introduce the foundational principles for a God-glorifying sex life. That's right: the way that you love your spouse can and should please the Lord. Learning and practicing the foundational principles presented in this book will pay *wonderful* dividends over the course of your marriage. And for those blessed with many years of marriage, I pray that God will use this book to deepen your commitment to loving your spouse well. Regardless of how long you have been married, you do not have the luxury of thinking that you have it all figured out. You will never graduate beyond learning how to love your spouse excellently.

God wants you to experience the very best of what He intended for sexual intimacy. God wants to bless your marriage in every conceivable way. He wants to cause your marriage to flourish and bless many other marriages. He wants to strengthen the covenant you made with your spouse before God. He wants the delights of your bedroom to fortify you against the temptations in the world. He wants you to taste the goodness of God's gift so that you never settle for the counterfeit pleasure that the world offers. God wants you to be captivated with His grace and goodness as you enjoy the precious gift of sexual intimacy.

Sex is such a natural desire. So natural, in fact, that we don't think of it as something that we need to work on. But sometimes things that are natural require some effort. Talking, for example, is one of the most natural things on the planet. Yet when it comes to public speaking, that very natural thing called "talking" requires an incredible amount of strategic planning and execution. Not too long ago, I was asked to offer up a prayer at the beginning of one of the President's speaking engagements. I wasn't asked to give a sermon or speech, just a two-minute prayer. But that two-minute prayer required a substantial amount of preparation. I had just two minutes to work in a number of components that were all appropriate for the occasion. Of course, I wanted to praise God for who He is. More than anything, I wanted to explain the gospel in the clearest of terms using Scripture—and to do so in a manner that conveyed that Jesus is the only way. With thousands of people in attendance, I was not about to leave out a clear explanation of the gospel. Talking is definitely natural, but this incredible opportunity required careful planning and effective execution.

Yes, sex, too, is natural. But that does not mean that you won't benefit from being intentional in how you love your spouse.

Even the slightest level of intentionality can produce incredible results in the area of sexual intimacy. Don't just let it happen or let it not happen in your marriage. Don't just let it happen in whatever way it happens to happen. Strive for the kind of happening that makes you want to make it happen more often. Be willing to work toward a greater sexual relationship with your spouse. There are no downsides, and the potential upside is something that you absolutely do not want to miss out on. Not only will you experience all that God intended sex to be, you also will find the pleasures of a strong and satisfying marriage. Beyond the joys of a flourishing relationship, God will use your marriage as a source of great encouragement to others. Are you willing to try just a little bit harder? Are you willing to devote more time and energy to sex? Are you willing to work toward understanding your spouse's needs? Are you willing to get out of your old rut and work on establishing some new habits? Are you willing to learn from the Bible about how God intended sexual intimacy to be enjoyed? Are you willing to pray for God to help you in this area of your life? If you are, then get ready for something very special!

How Do I Use This Book?

Read It Together. The most important thing is that you and your spouse participate in this study as a couple. It's not reasonable to expect a dramatic improvement in your sex life when only one of you is invested in the process. It takes two. Remember: the Scripture is the driving force behind *Sex Is . . . .* The principles derived from Song of Solomon form the basis for every chapter in this book. As such, start by reading God's Word. *Sex Is . . .* is about studying what God Almighty has to say on the subject. At the start of every chapter, ask God to speak to you, then read the assigned chapter from Song of Solomon. Then, having read the Scripture, read the corresponding chapter of this book. If you can, I recommend taking turns reading each chapter aloud. If this won't work for you, then read the chapter independently. Each chapter will explore powerful keys to experiencing a wonderful sex life. You might even think about highlighting portions of the book that resonate with you. This will give your spouse an opportunity to know what's going on in your heart and what you are learning. In some cases, you might highlight areas that you want your spouse to pay special attention to. In the back of the book, I have included an appendix entitled "Managing Disproportionate Desires." If you are currently experiencing disproportionate desires in your marriage, you might benefit from starting with the appendix. This will give you some practical tools to help you as you begin your journey through this book. After you have finished reading each chapter, it's time to talk about sex!

Do Your Homework. Unlike your dreaded assignments growing up, I promise you, you will not want to avoid the homework. These are not your typical assignments. This will be the most satisfying homework you have ever done. At the conclusion of each chapter, I will challenge you to discuss openly and honestly the lessons presented. It might be fun for some and awkward for others, but regardless of how it feels, I promise it will prompt eye-opening exchanges that will help you become better lovers. Expect some surprises! You may be tempted to skip these questions, but *I dare you* to answer them with transparency. Force yourselves through the blushing and the giggles so you can learn more about each other. Don't think for a minute that you have your spouse completely figured out. Even if you have been married for many years, you still have much to learn. As you discuss, remember to be sensitive and gentle with your spouse. Sexual intimacy is a very tender and delicate subject that must be approached with the greatest care and concern for your spouse. Use these conversations to affirm and encourage what you love about your spouse and to grow in the areas where you need improvement.

There will also be specific applications that I will challenge you and your spouse to act on. We are accustomed to striving in other areas of our life, but when it comes to our love life, we can be tempted to accept a status quo. Do your best to complete each assignment. You won't get a grade on the homework, but successful completion of these assignments has built-in rewards that you do not want to miss. What do you have to lose? Your marriage is worth the effort! After you've had an opportunity to discuss these thought-provoking questions, then I encourage you to pray together as a couple.

Pray Together. At the conclusion of each chapter, I include a prayer that can serve as a guide for your prayer time. The main thing is that you pray as a couple about these critical issues in your marriage. When was the last time that you prayed together about sex? God will help you love each other as you lean on Him for help. Without God you cannot accomplish anything, and that includes loving your spouse magnificently. You cannot transform your sex life through sheer determination. Instead, it will be a direct result of God's wondrous work in your marriage.

Make a Commitment. If you are serious about improving intimacy in your marriage, I challenge you to sign the covenant at the very end of the book. It's not about achieving perfection; this is not attainable. Instead, the marriage covenant is about formalizing your commitment to be the spouse that God has called you to be. It's about prioritizing your marriage as something worthy of working on. As you will read in the pages to follow, intimacy is about strengthening and unifying your marriage so that you will be more effective for the cause of the Lord Jesus Christ.

Chapter 1

SEX IS WONDERFUL

Scripture Reading: Song of Solomon 1

Amazing, sensational, breath-taking, exciting, awesome, incredible, pleasurable, overwhelming, delightful, thrilling. Sex is all of these and oh so much more. Words fail us in trying to describe the splendor of God's gift of sexual intimacy. What word would you use? I am choosing "wonderful"! There is a glorious wonder in sex that defies the greatest attempts to describe it. You cannot read Song of Solomon and conclude that sex between a husband and wife is anything but wonderful. The gift of sex is not just okay or second rate; it is wonderful. Sex is so wonderful, in fact, that it does not even have to be wonderful to be wonderful; it's just wonderful. Normally, people feel differently about what makes a great gift. We all have different tastes, interests, and hobbies. What you consider to be a great gift might miss the mark with the next person. But, when it comes to sex, there is overwhelming agreement that it is a wonderful thing. This universal truth transcends cultures and time periods. Only God could give a gift so magnificent that billions of people throughout history could resoundingly agree on as being intrinsically wonderful. There's no need to try to convince anybody. People get it: sex is wonderful.

Without question, the world has perverted the gift of sex into something that God never intended it to be. To most people in our world, sex is not the physical expression of an enduring love with a person you are committed to for the rest of your life. Instead, sex has become a narcissistic pursuit of pleasure. This idolatrous understanding of sex has led to deviant behaviors too depraved to enumerate. As people hurl themselves recklessly toward pleasure, they only find emptiness. Their emptiness leaves them more desperate than they were before. They take their unfulfilled longing for satisfaction to new and dangerous levels of sexual deviance in compulsive ways that lead to shame. This degrading spiral of behavior leads to unspeakable pain and brokenness, to the delight of Satan, who longs to destroy marriages. The pain experienced by so many, however, is only symptomatic of deviant expressions of sexuality. God's gift of sexual intimacy is "wonderful." Let's explore the splendor of this wonderful gift.

Wonderfully Beautiful

Song of Solomon is rich with botanical imagery. Their longing to delight themselves in love coincides with the blossoms appearing in the countryside (2:12). Did you know that a flower represents the reproductive function of plants? Think about that for a moment. The most beautiful expression of a plant (the flower) contains the reproductive functions. In the very same way, God has allowed the beautiful gift of sexual intimacy to be the mechanism He uses to fill the earth. And, just like a flower, it is beautiful!

The beautiful nature of sexual intimacy demands beautiful language. The splendor of this magnificent gift prompts some of the most colorful expressions in all of Scripture. These lovers weave provocative imagery into soaring rhetorical flourishes in order to communicate the force of their passion for each other. They summon glorious images that intermingle colors, textures, and metaphors to convey the intensity of their delight in each other. They invoke every sense in describing the ecstasy of their intimate relationship. Only God could give something so incredibly beautiful.

Wonderfully Pleasurable

Dare I say the obvious? Sex is wonderfully pleasurable. To ignore the physically pleasing aspect of intimacy would be to ignore Song of Solomon altogether. The lovers in Song of Solomon experience such incredible pleasure that it drives them to ignore even the most basic human needs. They joyfully give up sleep at the prospect of having sex with each other (2:17; 4:6). Even the basic need to eat serves the limited purpose of giving her strength to make love to her husband, as she says, "Strengthen me with raisins, refresh me with apples, for I am faint with love" (2:5). He feels the same way and would far rather feast on her, his "honeycomb" (5:1). Their desire to make love also eclipses any desire they might otherwise have for the finest wine. She says, "for your love is more delightful than wine" (1:2). She longs to intoxicate herself with his mouth and to give him "spiced wine to drink" from the nectar of her "pomegranates." I'll leave you with your imagination on that one, but for now consider how glorious the pleasure must be for these lovers to forego these basic human needs.

Wonderfully Overwhelming

In nearly every area of our lives, we loathe feeling overwhelmed. Nobody likes to feel overwhelmed when it comes to laundry, finances, or their job. But when it comes to sexual intimacy, few would rebuff what these lovers experience. The anticipation of expressing their love intimately is enough to overtake them in marvelous ways. She is completely overwhelmed with passion for her husband and exclaims twice that she is "faint with love" (2:5; 5:8). As she waits for him naked on her bed, her heart begins to pound with excitement (5:4). You don't hear them talking about other pleasures in this book. Every other pleasurable sensation takes a back seat to the intense satisfaction that they find in each other. When was the last time you felt this way about your spouse? Don't ever give up on the prospect of experiencing the very best of what God intended sexual intimacy to be.

Wonderfully Refreshing

We live in a world saturated with sin, pain, and violence. Our world is filled with unspeakable hardship. It seems every news cycle is punctuated with horrific acts against the most vulnerable. To varying degrees, we have all experienced pain and hardship in life. We have been mocked, disrespected, and ignored by others. We all know what it's like to feel afraid and anxious. We know what the sting of rejection feels like. We have all experienced loneliness and despair. We have faced disappointments and the pain of sudden tragedy. We have experienced financial pressure and the stress of demanding jobs. Sexual intimacy with your spouse is a sweet oasis from the pain and hardship of life. In the arms of your lover, you are treasured and adored. In the arms of your lover, you are reminded of God's amazing, unconditional love for you . . . a love that is bigger than all your faults and flaws. In this dark and cruel world, God has allowed you the joy of experiencing something so sweet, so beautiful, and so gentle. God has given you the privilege of drawing close to your spouse in what might otherwise be a very lonely world. The gift of sexual intimacy provides immeasurable joy as we journey through a life fraught with hardship.

Wonderfully Simple

Consider for a moment the uniqueness of this incredible gift. Unlike so many pleasurable activities in life, sexual intimacy is gloriously simple. Have you ever noticed that commercials are always selling pleasure for a price? If you buy their product, then you can experience a thrill, relaxation, adventure, or whatever else they may be selling. Worldly pleasure, however, is not so easily experienced for any length of time, unless escalated to cost-prohibitive levels. There is always a cost to worldly pleasure. Sexual intimacy with your spouse is gloriously anomalous in this way. These lovers in Song of Solomon need nothing but each other. They aren't looking for some tawdry stimulation to "spice up" their love life; they just want each other. There is nothing on earth that could intensify their love for each other. They don't need money, power, or possessions. Their sex life is not contingent on having a big house, or any house, for that matter. In fact, they seem quite content to make love underneath fir and cedar trees on a bed of greenery. Isn't it refreshing to see that a healthy sex life requires no stimuli beyond that of your lover? If God has blessed you with the joy of marriage, you also have the privilege of experiencing the simple wonder of sexual intimacy as He intended it.

Wonderfully Complete

Sexual intimacy engages positively every aspect of your being. We see how wonderfully complete the gift of sexual intimacy is as we read about the lovers in Song of Solomon. Their minds are engaged with thoughts of one another. Their lips (4:3, 11), their cheeks (1:10), and even their voices (2:14) are actively involved in their physical relationship. Even his taste buds are pleased with the "milk and honey" lying under her tongue (4:11; 7:8). Their noses are also busy, taking in the pleasant fragrances of each other. To entice her husband, she beckons the wind: "Awake, north wind, and come, south wind! Blow on my garden, that its fragrance may spread everywhere. Let my lover come into his garden and taste its choice fruits" (4:16). With his arms he embraces her (2:6; 8:3) and with his hands he takes hold of her breasts (7:8). I could go on, but I think you get the picture. They engage their entire bodies in enjoying the kind of pleasure that no other activity under heaven can emulate. It's not just that they are both feeling good but also that they are simultaneously enjoying wonderful gratification. But it's not just body parts that they intermingle.

These lovers intertwine even their hearts as they pursue each other sexually. To the core of their being, they desire intimacy with each other. The wife even describes her lover as "the one my heart loves" (3:1–4). He feels the same way and confesses that she has "stolen" his heart (4:9). She's not merely a sexual outlet for him, but the woman who owns his heart. The palpable longing keeps her awake when he is away, and the sound of his return makes her heart begin to pound (5:2, 4). The intermingling of their hearts fuels their wild physical passion for each other.

This is one of the reasons why marriage gets sweeter with time. As I reflect on my relationship with Stephanie, I can say with great confidence that we love each other more today than we ever have. I'm not as young or fit as I was when we married. I have more wrinkles and far less hair, but I also have more love for Stephanie than ever before. The intermingling of our hearts through the years fuels our love for each other. Unlike other pleasures in life, sexual intimacy never has to stop.

Wonderfully Lasting

Over and over in popular songs I've heard the common refrain of "just one more night." Isn't it sad that anybody would be in the pathetic position of pleading for just one more night in bed? In marriage, there's no pleading for one more night (or at least there shouldn't be). In marriage, sex is not a one-time binge but a lifetime of physical enjoyment. In a healthy marriage there is a glorious predictability about your prospects to enjoy this gift over and over and over and over and over. . . . In marriage, sex is literally the gift that keeps on giving. The white-hot intensity of the lovers in Song of Solomon leads to the kind of satisfaction that leaves them wanting more and more. Yet somehow their insatiable appetite for each other leads to a glorious contentment.

The benefits of a healthy sex life endure far beyond the physical ability to make love to your spouse. The seasons of life do have a tendency to change. Sometimes these new seasons bring about unexpected changes to marriages. If sexual intimacy becomes impractical for a marriage at some point, the benefit from having loved well for many years remains. Even when a couple's sex life diminishes by necessity, it does not destroy the wonderful intimacy that God galvanized through years of loving well. The years of intimacy can enrich the marriage to the point where it flourishes even in the absence of sexual intercourse. The harvest of sexual intimacy can be enjoyed until death parts a husband and wife!

Wonderfully Content

It's sad for me to hear how so many people talk about marriage. For many, it's nothing more than a "prison" or a "ball and chain." Marriage is the thing that has stolen their freedom and ability to enjoy life. It represents the one thing keeping them from enjoying life as they once did, a covenant that has ushered them into the doldrums of a bland and boring adult life. That may be true for some, but it's definitely not true of the lovers in Song of Solomon. When the husband looks at his wife, he sees a woman who represents life. Gazing at her, he says, "You are a garden fountain, a well of flowing water streaming down from Lebanon" (4:15). She's not a stagnant pool of useless, smelly water, but a source of refreshment. He sees her as a fountain of fresh water that nourishes life in a bountiful garden. She enriches his life in a way that helps him flourish as a man. She does not drain him; she fuels him. He does not despise her as the one who keeps him chained to a banal existence.

His wife knows how he feels about her and says confidently, "Thus I have become in his eyes like one bringing contentment" (8:10). She loves being the woman who brings him contentment. The Hebrew word translated as "contentment" is *shalom* (שָׁלוֹם). In this context, the word conveys the kind of "completeness" that brings "satisfaction" to their marriage.[1]

Does your husband say the same thing about you? Does your wife say this about you? She is not an emotional drain to him. On the contrary, she labors to satisfy him in ways that no other person on the planet could.

One of the beautiful consequences of their contentment is that they have eyes for only each other. The husband, who might reasonably be tempted to look at other women, only desires his wife. Even if he had the option to be with queens and concubines, he would still just

---

1. HALOT, s.v. שָׁלוֹם

want his wife (6:8). She's not sending her husband into a tempting world on an empty sexual tank. She's not withholding herself from her husband or rationing his sexual enjoyment. On the contrary, she has enticed him into her garden and openly invited him to make love to her: "Let my beloved come into his garden and taste its choice fruits" (4:16). Consequently, he doesn't see other women as missed opportunities that he could have enjoyed were it not for his dull marriage. I can think of plenty of words to describe their marriage, but "dull" is not one of them. Their marriage is passionate, exciting, thrilling, adoring, pleasurable, and even adventurous, but not dull. He's not secretly fawning after other women or lusting after them in his heart. On the contrary, he sees his wife as a "lily among thorns" (2:2). No other woman compares to his wife. He literally has no reason to look elsewhere, because his wife is so eager to satisfy and bring him sexual contentment.

Her willingness to satisfy her husband encourages him to desire time with her. We hear about the husband "leaping across the mountains" and "bounding over the hills" in Song of Solomon. This husband sees a window of opportunity to spend special time with his wife and says, "Come with me" (4:8). He's not looking for more hang-out time with the guys or coming up with excuses for why he needs to stay late at the office night after night. He's not trying to score tickets to the next home game. You don't see the malaise that has swept over many men, leaving them lethargic and uninterested with their wife. With a powerful determination, he rushes to whisk her away so that they can be together. He wants to be with the woman who makes his sexual needs a priority. One thing is clear: he would never attach the notion of contentment to his wife if she neglected his physical needs. If she ignored him sexually, it would have brought him mounting frustration, disappointment, and bitterness.

Song of Solomon also makes it very clear that he brings contentment to his wife as well. He longs to talk to his wife because she is his treasure. She loves that he listens and responds to her. He's not rolling his eyes and ignoring her thoughts and feelings. She adores the man who would never minimize her needs in the relationship. She is satisfied with how he verbalizes his affection and attraction. She is quite content with the man who esteems her as the most important woman in his life. Sexual intimacy in a godly marriage promotes a life-giving contentment.

Wonderfully Busy

You ask almost anybody how they are doing, and many—without even thinking—will retort, "Busy." Life runs at a frenetic pace. At the end of the day, it is staggering to think about how many tasks I was involved in. Even on days when it seems that I have not accomplished much, I am still so busy. I know that you have felt this way as well. At times, I thank God that I am able to lead a full and energetic life. But other times my schedule leaves me feeling exhausted and stressed. Have you ever found yourself counting down the days until your next vacation? Have you started to hate your smartphone yet?

There is, however, a different kind of busyness all together. The kind of busyness that nobody will ever see. The kind of busyness you will never want a vacation from. The kind of busyness you don't need a break from on the weekend. The kind of busyness that only leaves you wanting more. Song of Solomon presents the body of Christ with a picture of a glorious busyness that promotes peace, not angst. In marriage there can be a spirited and lively set of activities that do not promote stress. In Song of Solomon, these lovers touch, caress, admire, embrace, kiss, seduce, and lure each other into a glorious busyness. From far away he travels, even over mountains to be with his wife (2:8). He does not want a simple date. He wants an entire night with his wife (2:17). Joyfully, they go without sleep to lavish each other with love. Even when she does sleep, she dreams of her beloved (3:1–4). They devote a massive amount of time to adoring each other. Back and forth, they exchange the most thoughtful and meticulous flattery imaginable. The result of this kind of busyness is their shared desire to spend even more time together. They invite each other to get away from it all so that they can devote more time and energy to each other (8:14).

Wonderfully Delightful

If you have been married for any length of time, you know that marriage can be very challenging. You have to work to serve each other. You labor to sacrifice your desires for the good of your marriage. At times you feel hurt and frustrated. You may also experience anger. You likely struggle to be the spouse that God has called you to be. The difficulties may even drive you to your knees in prayer. But marriage is not all hardship. There are so many beautiful joys along the way. One of these joys is sexual intimacy. God has given you the wonderful gift of sexual intimacy so you can also experience incredible delight in marriage. In Song of Solomon, the wife delights in the intimacy she shares with her husband, "Like an apple tree among the trees of the forest is my beloved among the young men. I delight to sit in his shade, and his fruit is sweet to my taste" (2:3). Her husband represents the most luscious fruit in an otherwise tasteless forest. She delights in her husband and he delights in her.

How Realistic Is Their Sex Life?

Some might think it's ridiculous to think that somebody could sustain the responsibilities of a stressful life and enjoy the kind of sexual relationship as these lovers. Skeptics might say, "I don't read about the kids screaming in the background or about how stressful his job is. With all this talk of glorious fragrances, where is the reality of messy diapers in their house?" or "Song of Solomon is just a story about young lovers. It's not realistic after many years of marriage." Is Song of Solomon an exposé of how great sex can be for newlyweds or a paradigm for every relationship? God wants marriages to experience the joy of this wonderful gift. The splendor of sex does not need to fade with time. Instead, sex has the potential of becoming more and more wonderful in marriage over time. In marriage, time is your friend, not your enemy. Here are a few factors that have the potential of sweetening your sexual intimacy over the years of marriage.

1. **Love grows stronger with time.** As your love for your spouse

grows, your ability to express that love improves. We will focus on the relationship between love and sex in marriage in chapter 5, but for now, just think of love as a powerful engine driving your desire for your spouse.

2. **Beautiful memories accumulate with time.** The longer you are married, the more memories that you share together. Even the hard times have a way of seasoning your sex life. Enduring difficult times teaches you how to treasure the person who stood by you through the storms.
3. **Your knowledge of your spouse grows with time.** You only thought you knew your fiancé before you married. In your first year of marriage, you were probably surprised by a wide range of things that you did not know. As wonderful as your honeymoon was, you did not know back then nearly what you know now. With time has come a wealth of useful information about your lover. You know what excites your spouse and makes them tick. You know what makes each other smile. The old saying "knowledge is power" is definitely the case when it comes to sexual intimacy.
4. **The longer you walk with Christ, the more selfless and sacrificial you learn to be.** Being selfless is not optional for those who long to experience the best of sexual intimacy. Your relationship with Christ will sharpen your ability to love your spouse intimately.
5. **The longer you are married, the more compatible you become.** God knew exactly what He was doing when He put you and your spouse together. He knew all of the ways in which your strengths would complement your spouse's weaknesses and vice versa. This healthy dependence on each other creates an incredible intimacy that grows over time. This compatibility carries over into the bedroom where you are able to enjoy each other to the fullest.
6. **Your friendship grows over time.** As chapter 6 explores, your

> sex life will improve as your friendship improves. The longer you are married, the stronger your friendship can become. So, far from ruining the possibility of sensational sex, a long marriage makes it a reality through a thriving friendship.

How realistic is this book? God's Word is always true and perfectly relevant for your life. So the truths of Song of Solomon will be as realistic as you strive for them to be in your marriage. They are as realistic as you pray for them to be in your marriage. If you follow the model given to you in God's Word, passionate intimacy can be a reality for you!

Recapturing the Wonder

Not only is the gift of sex wonderful, it is a gift that God wants married couples to enjoy. Don't you just love giving gifts? When you really know someone, you know exactly the kind of gift that will cause their face to light up with joy. The joy of seeing their reaction makes the cost worthwhile. Sex is not just a biological necessity for procreation; it's a wonderful gift that God wants you and your spouse to relish. This enjoyment of each other leads to a strong and unified marriage that is more effective for the cause of Christ in the world. But for many marriages, sexual intimacy has become a source of contention.

Song of Solomon does not describe the sex life common today where the wife simply tolerates her husband's "overactive" sex drive so he won't be grumpy. She does not roll her eyes with irritation every time he wants to make love to her. Sex with her lover is not a wearisome chore that she's too busy or exhausted to deal with. She does not use sex as a manipulative weapon to control her husband. On the contrary, she seems happy to forego sleep if it means making love to her husband. She doesn't throw in his face all of the needs he has failed to meet every time he hints at his desire to make love. She's definitely not manufacturing "headaches" to avoid the subject altogether. Instead, she actively pursues her husband sexually with the kind of glorious vengeance that would thrill any man to the core of his being.

Song of Solomon does not describe the sex life common today

where the husband ignores his wife's nonsexual needs while obsessing over his own physical desires. He's not displaying constant irritation with her throughout the day, then wondering why she never wants to have sex at night. The husband doesn't just want sex; he wants to be with his best friend. He's not bored with his wife or with how she looks; he lavishes his compliments on her. You also don't see him emotionally withdrawn from his wife in frustration with her unwillingness to give herself to him. Nor is he finding excuses every other night to hang out with the guys. Instead, he rushes toward her like a wild animal (2:8–9). He's not fawning after other women or mentally creeping his way into some dark fantasyland so that he can imagine what sex would be like with other women. He's not skulking around dark corners looking for a cheap thrill. No, she is the only woman for him, "like a lily among the thorns is my darling among the young women" (2:2). Their sex life has not been reduced to a bland physical act that they perform on a scheduled basis. Instead, we see an eruption of wild passion that drives them recklessly toward each other.

In any healthy marriage there will be a natural ebb and flow to the splendor of the physical relationship. The normal pressures of life and stress that so often accompany responsibility can hinder sexual intimacy. Without a doubt, a demanding job can, at times, throw cold water on your sexual relationship. And if you are blessed with children, you also battle fatigue. Dirty diapers, sleepless nights, and endless errands to care for these little ones can push you beyond exhaustion. Particularly for the wife, fatigue can be a major hurdle to enjoying a great sex life. There may be health challenges as well. When you or your partner don't feel well, sex may be the very last thing on your mind. There is no shortage of potential challenges to your love life.

Even in the best of marriages, it would be naïve and unrealistic to expect every sexual experience to represent yet another mountain peak of ecstasy. But that's not really the goal with sexual intimacy either. It's not like you are a gymnast trying to score a perfect 10 on the floor exercise routine. No relationship needs to feel the weight of some unattainable ideal. That's not what this book is about. I hope this takes the pressure off! Understanding the wonderful gift of sex is more about valuing and prioritizing something that your marriage needs. It's about the lifelong journey of loving your spouse well. As Gary Chapman notes, sex in marriage "is not static. We move in and out of intimacy based on our behavior toward each other."[2] This book is about strengthening your relationship with your spouse so that your marriage is more effective for the cause of Christ. It's about the never-ending task of learning more and more about your spouse.

Understanding that there will be challenges to overcome in your sex life is one thing, but being complacent is quite another.

To those who have resigned themselves to having a lackluster sex life, God says, "Sex is wonderful!" To those who have forgotten just how good sexual intimacy can be, God says, "Sex is wonderful!" To those who have made their spouse live underneath a sexual lockdown, God says, "Sex is wonderful!" To those who have fallen underneath Satan's temptation, God reminds us that "Sex with your spouse is wonderful!" To those who are too wounded to give themselves sexually to their spouse, God says, "Sex with your spouse is wonderful!" To those who think that they have experienced the splendor of the gift, God says, "Sex can be even *more* wonderful!" To those who have given up on the covenant of marriage altogether, God says, "Sexual intimacy in marriage is wonderful!"

God intends for His gift of sexual intimacy to be wonderful in your marriage. The splendor of this wonderful gift should evoke explosive praise in our hearts. But the reality is that many relationships struggle in this area. Maybe part of the reason for this is that so many are getting the wrong advice. The answers to a wonderful sex life won't be found in magazines that tout secrets to "mind-blowing" sexual encounters. You also won't find answers among those who are supposedly experts

---

2. Gary Chapman, *Now What: The Chapman Guide to Marriage after Children* (Carol Stream, IL: Tyndale, 2009), 61.

by virtue of their modeling or acting career (as though only beautiful people who have shown little discretion with their sexuality hold the keys to experiencing sex at its best). Hollywood movies that display graphic sexual encounters as ideals to be replicated are an equally absurd source of information. Rather predictably, they present sexual intimacy in a manner that is completely detached from reality. Movies that present sexual encounters with multiple uncommitted partners conveniently avoid the devastating consequences of sin. Hollywood depicts the wild romance of illicit encounters while ignoring the reality of emotional devastation, sexually transmitted diseases, and unwanted pregnancies.

Appealing to secular culture to understand God's gift of sex will only lead to more confusion and heartache. The only way to recapture the splendor of sexual intimacy is to study God's Word. God's Word tells the truth about sex and the truth about how it is best enjoyed. Do you believe that God is a credible witness when it comes to the issues of sexual intimacy? If you do, then it's time for you to allow God to speak truth into your marriage. It is God's Word that will lead to strong marriages, strong families, and strong churches.

Wonderful Intimacy and Strong Marriages

God will enrich and strengthen your marriage as you enjoy the splendor of a wonderful sex life. Intimacy in your marriage will help you remain captivated by your spouse. It will help you find joy in the valleys of life and through the difficult seasons of marriage. The wonderful gift of intimacy will help you become more resilient against the temptations of life. How can a man contemplate another woman when there is no other woman on the planet who has mastered the art of wonderful sex with him? Why would a woman fantasize about being with another man when her husband has been so careful to tenderly love and care for her? Sexual intimacy will help you prioritize your marriage above every other relationship in life. Sexual intimacy in a godly marriage will also cultivate gratitude in your heart toward the God who created this wonderful gift and gave you a partner to enjoy it with.

The remainder of this book is devoted to exploring ways you can experience the wonder of sexual intimacy in your marriage. As you begin this journey with your spouse, take a few moments to discuss openly and honestly the answers to the questions that follow.

Homework

1. What do you love most about your sex life? Finish this sentence: "I love it when you . . ."
2. In what ways have you taken this gift for granted?
3. Ask each other the following question: "What do I need to do to make sexual intimacy even more wonderful for you?"
4. As you begin this study on sexual intimacy, what is one thing you would like to learn about each other?
5. What would need to change about your schedule to make sex a greater priority in your marriage? Find something that you can eliminate from your schedule to improve your sex life.

A Prayer for You

"Father, you are the giver of good and perfect gifts. Thank you for the gift of sexual intimacy. Thank you for blessing me by giving me a wonderful spouse—a person that I can love intimately. You knew exactly what we would need when you brought us together.

"We confess that we have at times taken this for granted. Forgive us for not always taking the time to understand each other's intimate needs. Forgive us for overlooking each other's desires. Forgive us for all of the ways that we have grumbled about each other.

"In the very same way that you cause us to grow and learn in other areas, help us to grow in the area of serving each other sexually. Help us to understand all of the ways in which our sex life may fall short of what you want it to be. Help us to be earnest in the way that we care for each other sexually. Help us to be patient and giving even when we struggle to understand each other's physical needs. Teach us how to communicate openly with each other so that we can grow in this area of our marriage.

"May the love we have for one another show the world the difference that Jesus can make in a marriage. Overwhelm all our weaknesses and selfishness with a profound desire to love each other in ways that would bring contentment. Cause our sex life to live up to the beauty and wonder that we read about in Song of Solomon.

"As you strengthen our marriage, help us to partner more effectively in doing the things you have called us to do. Accomplish miraculous things through our small efforts! Help our marriage to reflect in some small way the magnificence of the love you displayed in sending Jesus to die for us on the cross. By the power that raised Jesus to new life, empower me to love my spouse. In Jesus' name, Amen."

Chapter 2

SEX IS DESIGNED

Scripture Reading: Song of Solomon 2

Would you ask a professional musician how to operate a nuclear submarine? Would you ask a professional basketball player how to genetically alter a vegetable to achieve maximum growth in a different climate? Of course not! Neither should you or I expect the world to know how to achieve the most meaningful sex life. An amazing sex life is not as intuitive as we might think. It is only God's design for sexual intimacy that works. God created the wonderful gift of sexual intimacy, and He is precisely the One who knows how it should be enjoyed.

Marriage

"And God saw that it was good." We hear this phrase over and over in Genesis 1 to characterize the magnificence of God's creation. From the beasts of the field and the fish of the ocean, everything that God created was intrinsically good. God is a masterful Creator. After the repeated references to all of the "good" that God created, Genesis 2 introduces the first thing in the Bible that was "not good." Do you know what that was? In Genesis 2:18, the Bible says, "It is not good for the man to be alone." So God responds by forming Eve out of the rib

He had taken out of man. Then, presenting the woman to Adam, God said, "That is why a man leaves his father and mother and is united to his wife and they become one flesh" (Gen. 2:24). Marriage between a man and a woman who are committed to each other for life is a good and wonderful gift of God. Song of Solomon is a beautiful example of this reality.

She says, "I am my beloved's and my beloved is mine" (6:3). She does not describe her lover as her "boyfriend" or her "friend with benefits." She doesn't say, "This is just a casual thing" or that "He just stays with me." They don't just hook up over long weekends. She is also not living the lie that he might marry her someday. She belongs to her lover and her lover belongs to her—they are married. Six times he refers to her as his bride.[1] There is a beauty in belonging totally and completely to your lover. And far from destroying their sexual relationship, their exclusive, committed relationship provides the ideal framework for them to express their sexuality. The exclusivity of their relationship acts like an incendiary device that fuels their passion for each other. Outside of this covenant, the Bible gives no license for sexual intimacy.

The wife actually expresses concern over and over for the younger women of Jerusalem, saying, "Daughters of Jerusalem, I charge you by the gazelles and by the does of the field: Do not arouse or awaken love until it so desires" (2:7; 3:5; 8:4). She is saying, in other words, that the day will come for them to enjoy the kind of relationship she's experienced. But until they are married, they should not arouse sexual intimacy. She feels so strongly about this that she overtly expresses her desire to protect young girls with "towers of silver" and "panels of cedar" until "the day she is spoken for" (8:8–9). What a beautiful reminder of how the church should care for young girls who are not ready to engage in sexual behavior. But she herself does not fall into the category of those who are not prepared to have intercourse. She

1. Song of Solomon 4:8, 9, 10, 11, 12; 5:1.

is not to be compared with the young girl whose breasts are not yet grown. With confidence she says, "my breasts are like towers. Thus, I have become in his eyes like one bringing contentment" (8:10).

The world thinks that when it comes to sex, the more deviant the better, but the Bible teaches the more *holy* the better. The world will say that they have sex figured out and that Christians will have to settle for something vanilla prescribed in the Bible. I don't know about you, but I don't see a bland and boring sex life as I read Song of Solomon. As Bill and Pam Farrel write, "The best sex is not found in Las Vegas or on some porn screen. No. The best of what sex is, the most wonderful examples of true fulfilling and passionate sexuality, is found inside the private bedroom walls of committed married couples."[2] Let's examine how sexual intimacy flourished within the loving bounds of a biblical marriage.

Sex in Marriage Can Be Uninhibited

Since they are bound safely within the covenant of marriage, the lovers in Song of Solomon are free to express their exuberant love for each other. Their natural inhibitions have been gloriously destroyed by the secure bond of marriage. Sex can never be this way in a dating or casual relationship. The uncertainty of the relationship and its propensity to unravel without any warning leave men and women vulnerable, guarded, and careful. Guarded and careful are not attitudes that promote incredible intimacy. In fact, the more a person gives sexually to an uncommitted partner, the more pain they will experience when their love is not returned. How could you ever be yourself in the bedroom if your lover has not made a commitment to you?

Outside of marriage, sexual relationships are marked by caution, fear, and apprehension. In the covenant of a godly marriage, you don't have to worry about what he might say to his friends after having gone to bed with you. "Is he going to make fun of me or laugh at me?" "Did

---

2. Bill and Pam Farrel, *Red-Hot Monogamy* (Eugene, OR: Harvest House, 2006), 14.

she think I was being sexy or ridiculous when I . . .?" These would be natural concerns among those who have sex outside of the covenant of marriage.

Do you hear any of this kind of apprehension or caution when these lovers in Song of Solomon talk about each other? Hear them in their own words:

> Your stature is like that of the palm, and your breasts like clusters of fruit. I said, "I will climb the palm tree and take hold of its fruit." May your breasts be like clusters of grapes on the vine, the fragrance of your breath like apples, and your mouth like the best wine (7:7–9).

Their exclusive marriage relationship has provided for them the perfect realm in which to intoxicate each other with love.

The covenant of marriage is not meant to stifle your sexuality but to encourage the safe and unfettered enjoyment of it. Within the covenant of marriage, you are free to express your love for your spouse. You are free to be exactly who God made you to be with your spouse. In marriage, your inhibitions can take a back seat to your overwhelming passion for your spouse. In marriage, you can relax underneath the safety of the covenant that you both made before God. So don't hold back. Cast yourself passionately toward each other in full confidence that you are safe within the covenant of marriage.

Sex in Marriage Is Smarter

We've seen the same scenario played over and over in the movies. Two people, with little attachment, throw caution to the wind and enjoy a wildly romantic night. The carefully crafted lines and overproduced pageantry would convince many that the fairy tale is real life and the kind of experience that can be replicated. Who are they kidding? It is patently ridiculous to think that you could sexually satisfy or be truly satisfied by a complete stranger. The idea that you could have incredible sexual encounters with a stranger is deceitful. More than likely, illicit sexual encounters turn into awkward blunders that leave both of you feeling empty and ashamed.

Sex becomes amazing over years of learning more and more about your spouse. Marriage provides the perfect framework to learn all about your lover. Over time you can learn the things your spouse likes and doesn't like. You know what to say and what not to say. You know how he wants you to dress and how she wants you to speak to her. You will know how and where to kiss each other. After years of giving yourselves to each other, you know exactly where to touch each other and what positions will provide the greatest satisfaction. Figuring all of that out in the span of a few minutes is an absurd proposition. Marriage provides a lifetime to learn how to indulge sexually in your spouse in a way that is mutually gratifying.

Sex in Marriage Is Free from Shame

In marriage, there is no waking up in the morning grieving your indiscretion when you have given yourself sexually. You won't be filled with emotional panic because of your vulnerability. You won't be afraid that he will try to make a discreet exit in the morning before you rouse from your sleep. You won't wonder who else he is doing those intimate acts with when he's not with you. You won't dread his empty politeness as he clumsily tries to tell you that it was a terrible mistake and that he does not want any kind of serious relationship. There will be no need to wonder if there is any possibility that you have contracted some sexually transmitted disease. You won't need to wait anxiously by the phone for him to call or desperately wait for him to "pop the question." You won't face the emotional devastation of giving yourself to someone who wants nothing to do with you. Instead, you will be able to say along with this young woman, "I have become in his eyes like one bringing contentment" (8:10).

Sex in Marriage Is Not Rationed

Marriage is not a paradigm for intermittent sexual encounters between a husband and wife. Instead, it is meant to provide the sole realm in which both partners consistently meet each other's needs. The Bible actually commands those who are married not to stop having sex, saying, "The husband should fulfill his marital duty to his wife, and likewise the wife to her husband" (1 Cor. 7:3). The Greek word translated "duty" elsewhere in Scripture is used to refer to a financial debt. In the minds of most people, debt is not a great thing; in fact, it's typically something that you want to get rid of as fast you as can. But Paul speaks of a more glorious kind of debt that you will never pay off, nor will you ever want to pay it off. This debt is the responsibility you have to supply the sexual needs of your spouse. In no uncertain terms, Paul writes, "Do not deprive each other except by mutual consent and for a time, so that you may devote yourselves to prayer. Then come together again so that Satan will not tempt you because of your lack of self-control" (1 Cor. 7:3, 5). You should not withhold yourself because ultimately your body does not belong to you alone but also to your spouse (1 Cor. 7:4). So absent the conditions that might lead to a very temporary withholding of yourself, Paul says, don't stop giving yourself to your spouse.

Do you see the incredible advantage the marriage covenant has over fornication? Unlike illicit sexual encounters, sex within marriage is not something you need to moderate. There is no hiding, sneaking around, or trying to stop. Instead, God invites you to enjoy your spouse to the utmost. The glorious irony is that every attempt to satisfy ourselves only leads to a desire for more of our spouse. At some point, you might want to say to the happily married couple in Song of Solomon, "Enough, already! Surely you have had enough." But their passion for each other escalates far beyond what can be experienced outside the covenant of marriage. The more passion you have for your spouse, the more passion you will have for your spouse. The more you make love to your spouse, the more you will want to make love to your spouse. This explains how marriage after many years grows more passionate.

Sex in Marriage Is Safe

Safe sex is not condoms and birth control. Safe sex is what happens within the wonderful covenant called marriage. Outside of the covenant of marriage, there is no such thing as safe sex. So let's talk about breaking boundaries and pushing the limits for a moment. I suppose these concepts can evoke wonderful images of shattering glass ceilings and achieving the extraordinary. But breaking certain barriers can lead to catastrophe. When Hurricane Katrina battered the southern coast of the United States, it caused over fifty breaches in the levees designed to protect the city of New Orleans. As a result, over 80 percent of the city flooded, leaving death and destruction in its wake. Still today, the city has not fully recovered from the devastation. The compromised boundary brought a catastrophe.

Here's another example. Did you know that NASCAR requires restrictor plates on their race cars? Without these restrictor plates, the cars would accelerate at speeds above 220 mph and lift into the stands. The restrictor plate provides a helpful, life-saving boundary. Think of marriage as a loving boundary that God established for sexual intimacy.

Ignoring God's design for marriage will lead to unbelievable pain and heartache. For all the talk of safe sex in our world today, you can be sure of one thing. Sex outside the covenant of marriage is never safe. Why do we think that we can ignore boundaries and remain unscathed from the calamity they are meant to protect us from? Many who thought they were liberating themselves from the unreasonable restraints of an antiquated institution have only found bondage to shame, guilt, and, in some cases, sexually transmitted diseases. There is no sexual freedom or satisfaction in syphilis, HIV, hepatitis B, HPV, or cervical cancer. There is no freedom in a broken heart. Sin never liberates, it always enslaves. Even still, our fallen world continues to push the narrative that monogamy destroys sexual expression and that you can only find satisfaction when you engage in fleeting encounters between multiple uncommitted partners. What an absurd thought.

I don't think I will ever forget the stinging anger I saw in one husband's eyes as he and his wife sat in my office trying to cope with the devastation of her affair. After many years of marriage, their relationship was unraveling beyond the point of repair. I would have done almost anything to save their marriage, but the damage was done. After exhausting a few last-ditch attempts, they divorced and the family was forever broken. I wonder how painful it must have been for her to look into the eyes of her children. Only time will tell how her affair will affect her family for generations.

God does not want you to experience this pain, so He warns us over and over in the Bible to avoid sexual immorality. From cover to cover, a compelling refrain arises out of the Bible, as though God is pleading with you, "Don't commit sexual sin!"

God commands believers through the apostle Paul in Colossians, saying, "Put to death, therefore, whatever belongs to your earthly nature: sexual immorality, impurity, lust, evil desires and greed, which is idolatry" (Col. 3:5). No matter what, "the marriage bed [should be] kept pure, for God will judge the adulterer and all the sexually immoral" (Heb. 13:4). God put the matter so plainly in the Ten Commandments when He said, "You shall not commit adultery" (Exod. 20:14). Christians never have to wonder what God's will is when it comes to sexual sin. God's will is always so patently clear. According to 1 Thessalonians 4:3, "It is God's will that you should be sanctified: that you should avoid sexual immorality." All sin is alike in that it is a deviation from God's holy standard. All sin deserves punishment. All sin needs forgiveness. So in several categories sin is all the same. But God clearly separates sexual sin from every other sin in the Bible. The apostle Paul writes, "Flee from sexual immorality. All other sins a person commits are outside the body, but whoever sins sexually, sins against their own body" (1 Cor. 6:18).

Be a Locked Garden to the World

> You are a garden locked up, my sister, my bride; you are a spring enclosed, a sealed fountain (4:12).

When he looks at his bride, he sees a utopian-like garden full of the most beautiful and fragrant flowers and spices. But to the rest of the world, she is a "locked garden." He knows that there is no possibility of her allowing anybody else into her garden. Godly women today need to make the same choice to remain a locked garden to those they are not married to. The only man who has the key to her garden is her husband.

Since they are married, she invites him into her garden, saying, "Let my beloved come into his garden and taste its choice fruits" (4:16). If you invite your husband into your garden, I can tell you right now how he will respond: *He will show up.* And that's precisely what the very next verse says: "I have come to my garden—my sister, my bride. I gather my myrrh with my spices. I eat my honeycomb with my honey. I drink my wine with my milk . . ." (5:1). He goes down to her garden because it belongs to him too. This is what 1 Corinthians 7:4 is talking about when it says, "The wife does not have authority over her own body but yields it to her husband. In the same way, the husband does not have authority over his body but yields it to his wife." Almost nothing will keep your husband from coming to you when you invite him into your garden.

Unfortunately, many married women don't give their husbands access to their garden. If you don't invite your husband into your garden, he will very likely become pent up with irritation, frustration, and anger (we'll return to this topic later). Ladies, be a locked garden to the world, but give the key to your husband for him to enjoy regularly.

Keep the Boundary Intact

You will not enjoy the fullness of what God intends for you sexually if you are not completely faithful to your spouse. Marriage does not insulate you from sexual temptation. Satan will try to lure you away from your spouse with the false promise of sexual ecstasy. But the reality is that he will only succeed in destroying your chances of ever experiencing it. Unfaithfulness to your spouse will lead to unspeakable pain. So how can we withstand sexual temptation?

Christians are not supposed to run from much in the Christian life. The Bible teaches us to be strong and courageous (Josh. 1:9) and that the righteous are as bold as a lion (Prov. 28:1). Even when facing the devil, the Bible teaches us to resist him so that he will flee (James 4:7). We do not back down, we don't give up, and we never run . . . except when it comes to one thing—sexual immorality! Don't be brave. Don't test your ability to withstand temptation. Don't try out your powers of self-control; just run. This is precisely what the apostle Paul teaches in 1 Corinthians 6:18: "Flee from sexual immorality." Run just as Joseph did when Potiphar's wife tried desperately to seduce him into bed (Gen. 39). As you run from every form of sexual sin, God will give you victory!

Even without committing the physical act of adultery, you can wound your exclusive relationship with your spouse. Many people have emotional affairs. An emotional affair happens when you regularly share your innermost thoughts and feelings with somebody you are not married to. Your spouse is the only person of the opposite sex that you should be sharing your emotions with. These emotional attachments can form so quickly and can lead to powerful temptation. Are you having regular lunches with a coworker that are becoming increasingly personal? Are you trying to strike up a friendship with an old boyfriend or girlfriend online? Do you find yourself texting inappropriate things to somebody whom you keep saying is "just a friend"? Though you might be able to summon the mental gymnastics necessary to rationalize this foolish behavior, your spouse will see all the way through to your wandering heart. And they will feel betrayed. The fact that they will respond by withholding themselves sexually from you will be the least of your worries.

Are you struggling with the sin of pornography? More and more people are silently killing their marriages through Internet pornography. The accessibility of graphic sexual images through smartphones has made this one of the most pressing moral issues in our culture. And it is no longer just a man's issue; more and more women are turning to Internet pornography. One Barna study reported that one-third of women twenty-five and under seek out pornography on a monthly basis compared to 67 percent of men.[3] If you are struggling with addiction to pornography, I want you to know that there is forgiveness and hope for all who are ready to turn from their sin. I encourage you to confess your sin, seek an accountability partner, and reach out to a minister or counselor for help.

When it comes to keeping the boundaries for your marriage intact, you also need to be careful about how you look at and think about members of the opposite sex. Are your casual glances at other women turning into stares? Or do you catch yourself leering at women when you are in public? Is your thought life becoming increasingly consumed with thoughts of other women or men? Though you may console yourself, saying that you've not done anything, remember the words of Jesus, "But I tell you that anyone who looks at a woman lustfully has already committed adultery with her in his heart" (Matt. 5:28). There is not a person alive who has not struggled to some degree in their life with this. Every person will face temptation in this arena. The main thing is that you are leaning on God to empower you to live above a sexually impure thought life. You cannot do this on your own.

Others harm the beauty of their exclusive relationship by threatening to leave their spouse. You will not soon recover from the bruising, emotional blow of threatening to walk away from your spouse. Needless to say, such threats do not lead to passionate sexual encounters with your spouse. Instead, these harmful words will teach them to withhold themselves sexually out of self-preservation. If you have done or said anything to make your spouse think you might leave, confess your sin and ask for forgiveness. When you are in the middle of an argument, guard your mouth from ever saying anything to make your spouse feel like you might just walk away.

---

3. David Kinnaman, "The Porn Phenomenon," Barna Group, February 5, 2016, https://www.barna.com/the-porn-phenomenon/.

"BRUISED AND BLESSED"

"Many may ask why I stayed with a serial adulterer of the heart—or why he stayed with a woman who belittled him daily. During most of our marriage, pornography crept up like a demon and devoured what happiness we had managed to gain. Pornography is like a drug that destroys the attitudes of a husband and wife. On this drug, my kind, loyal, generous, and brave husband became overtly angry, betraying, selfish, and cowardly. And as for me? I had always planned to be loving—admiring, even—toward my husband. I would be his greatest support, his resting place, and we would help each other grow in faith. But utter disgust replaced whatever admiration I had for him. I made our home a place he feared to be, and the faith I wanted to grow quickly dwindled into a burning anger mingled with a drowning sorrow. How could God have allowed me to end up where I was?

"We daily chipped away each other's worth. Here is the truth: if someone asked me, even now, if they should stay in the situation we were in, I could not encourage them to do so. My conscience would destroy me for it. In the long run, I stayed because God changed us.

"Last year, I determined that my husband could live with this demon . . . but I did not have to. I felt no requirement to stay based on our vows, because he had broken them—a position I made known. When he relapsed again, I packed a bag and moved out. I made this choice because I realized that I had one. In this way I took responsibility for my actions rather than blaming God and my husband for the position I was in.

"At first, it was very rough being away from my husband. I missed all the good and wonderful things about him. But at the same time, staying felt like enabling him. I was done allowing his problem to govern my life.

"During my time away, I gained a new understanding of God's love for us, and of how sin damages our relationship with Him. I never stopped wanting the best for my husband. I wouldn't admit it at some points, but I loved him still. I missed having fellowship with him. He did not become 'un-precious' to me, and I deeply desired for his healing, *not for his shame.* If a human is capable of this love and pain, how much more does God love and ache for His children, desiring healing and joy for us? For me? Yet, time and time again, I have rejected God's love, peace, and fellowship by holding on to my bitterness and shame.

"This thought broke a wall I had steadily built up for nearly my entire life. I had listened to the lie that I was unloved, small, worthless, and even a mistake. God overcame this wall and called me closer to Him. The most unnatural peace overcame me. I became convinced that I was a loved child of God. This led me to ask how I should be treating my husband.

"God wanted to show love to him and remind him that he was God's child too. First Peter 3:7 calls spouses 'heirs together of the grace of life.' I decided to treat my husband as such. When he was angry, I chose to see his pain, driving to the apartment just to hug him and let him know I saw his hurt. I could not do this in my own strength, because I had no love to give before. Though I was defenseless, I now had God's strength. I no longer saw my husband as pitiful and small—now I saw him as God's child, a man who had forgotten who he was, who was hurting more than he knew how to express.

"I was gone for six weeks. After the roughest two weeks, my husband began to show what he valued by consistently rejecting temptation. I began to see peace and honor return to him. I saw a healthy pride come back. I saw his focus slowly shift from shame to healing. He began to respect me as well. Love without respect is not a love worth having. Love does not diminish value; it holds it up. Love does not enable destruction; it stands against it. But neither does love abandon. Though my husband and I were apart, we continued to walk alongside each other, strengthening one another. Because love inspires and requires more from each of us.

"I would be lying if I said our marriage is always easy. Yes, sometimes we allow the past to haunt our present. But when you think about it, we have been collecting scars our entire life.

"Now we are working toward understanding where those scars exist, being careful not to poke and prod at each other's wounds. We are working towards encouraging each other in our walk with God, in our work, in our education, and more. We value our marriage enough to make a monetary investment in it; we go to therapy weekly. My husband opens my car door, finding contentment in trying to make me feel special; I let him, rather than doing it myself to show him that I don't need him. When he has an interview, I trust his judgment and abilities. I encourage him, take pride in him, and admire the confidence he has both in his own abilities and in God's timing. When I feel my studies are too much and I'll never do enough, he pushes me to own my successes and encourages me not to give up. We are learning to believe in each other and in our marriage. But mostly we are learning to believe that God is never far off . . . that He loves us, values us, and is rooting for us. That He loves us in a way that will never abandon, because He so loves us.

"In short, to describe my husband and me, we are bruised, we are blessed . . . and we are His."

—Married Eight Years

Broken Boundaries, Broken Families, Broken Churches

It's not just about the devastation that sexual sin will cause in your marriage. If you allow the boundaries of your marriage to be compromised, those you love the most will suffer the most. You may be willing and able to go through a rough patch in your marriage, but will your children fare as well? You cannot predict all of the ways that your sin might devastate your children. Will they develop a substance abuse problem? Will they struggle with depression? Will they follow your example and start experimenting sexually? Will they act out in criminal ways that forever damage their future? Only time will tell. Sexual sin in your marriage can affect your family for generations to come. It's not possible to wrap your mind around every negative consequence that could come as a result of sexual sin. God's forgiveness and grace are available for all who turn from their sin. But this forgiveness does not erase the painful consequences for our actions.

Sexual sin in marriage also has the potential of causing significant damage to the body of Christ. I cannot think of a category of sin more devastating to the body of Christ than sexual immorality. Sexual sin can produce irreparable fault lines in churches that end up collapsing entire ministries. Do you love your brothers and sisters in Christ enough to maintain the boundary lines of your marriage?

In short, sexual sin has the potential of hurting everybody you love. As you fortify the boundaries of your marriage and seek to love your spouse well, God will bless your family and strengthen your church. Strong marriages provide an endless stream of blessings for your children and your church. Ask God what you need to do, to fortify your marriage relationship against the temptation of the Evil One. Invite God to change anything and everything about how you interact with others at work and in the community for the sake of your family and your church. Seek wise counsel from Christian couples that you respect on the best ways to avoid compromising the boundaries that protect your marriage.

We're Married . . . Where's the Great Sex?

Marriage itself does not produce amazing sex. In fact, it may produce no sex at all. Instead, the marriage covenant provides the realm in which to love your spouse magnificently. The covenant of marriage gives you the opportunity to love and serve your spouse more than any other person on the planet can. Marriage also presents you with the opportunity to pray for your spouse and invest in their well-being. Marriage is the commitment to give your spouse more attention than anybody else will. It is the pledge to cultivate eyes only for them.

Struggling with intimacy in your marriage may be a sign of having divided affections. Your wife will know if you love your friends more than her. She will know if you love your job more than her. She will know if you love your hobby more than her. She will know by how you spend your time, your energy, and your money. She will know by how you look at her or by whether you even look at all. She will know by whether or not you take her phone calls and return her text messages. She will know by how you spend your weekends. She will know by how you speak to her and whether or not you listen to her. She will know by how you look at other women in the grocery store. She will know if your heart is not exclusively glued to her. She can smell your divided heart from a mile away, and it grieves her and leaves her cold toward you in the bedroom.

In the same way, your husband notices when you don't care to look beautiful for him anymore. He can tell by how you talk to him whether or not you value his opinion and respect him. He can hear your disapproval and judgment in your voice. He might not be the most observant person, but he definitely notices how enthusiastic you can be when it comes to everything but sex. He notices when you would rather talk to your friends on the phone than with him. He watches as you give your time and attention to everything and everybody but him.

One of the best ways to keep the boundary lines in your marriage strong is to cultivate eyes for only your spouse. There is no way to protect your marriage from harm if your eyes are consistently darting to and from other people in life that you find attractive. Sexual intimacy cannot flourish in an environment where you spend more time thinking about others than you do your spouse. I think that we can all agree that this would be a wonderful thing, but, practically speaking, how do we do it? Here some practical suggestions to cultivating eyes for only your spouse.

1. **Spend time each day giving thanks to God for your spouse.** Thank God for all of the ways your spouse cares for you. As you do this, God will change the way that you look at and interact with your spouse. God is the One who can help you cultivate eyes for only your spouse.
2. **Purpose to spend time each day thinking about your spouse.** The more you think about your spouse, the more you will want to

think about your spouse. The less you think about your spouse, the less you will want to think about your spouse. The more you think about your spouse, the less mental space you will have to entertain temptation. Take time to think back to the last time you made love to your spouse. Your thought life will create a wonderful trajectory that your actions are likely to follow.

3. **Plan your next romantic adventure with your spouse.** Sometimes having something to look forward to helps us to think longingly about our spouse. Dream about your next romantic date night or adventurous rendezvous. The more you include your spouse into your future plans, the more that you will be able to treasure them in the present.
4. **Treat your spouse like a treasure.** One of the best ways to cultivate eyes for only your spouse is to devote time lavishing love on them. The more you treasure your spouse, the more they will treasure you. As your spouse begins to treasure you, it will become increasingly natural to think more and more about them. It's pretty hard not to think about someone who is treating you like royalty.

If you are ready for great sex in your marriage, start by making sure that the boundary lines of your marriage are intact. A divided heart is the enemy of great sex in a marriage. When two people love each other exclusively within marriage, God inflames their passion for each other. Treasure your spouse more than any other human being on the planet. Put your spouse first before everybody else. Think more about your spouse than anybody else. Spend more time with your spouse than anyone else. Serve your spouse more than anyone else. Support your spouse more than anyone else. Pray for your spouse more than anyone else. Love your spouse more than anyone else. As you begin to recapture the exclusivity of your marriage, the passion can return with incredible force!

Homework

1. Take a moment and share with each other what first attracted you to each other.
2. Take turns completing the following sentence: "The greatest thing about our marriage is . . ."
3. Ask each other the following question: "What can I do to make you feel more confident and uninhibited in the bedroom?"
4. Discuss whether anything in your marriage has the potential of damaging the exclusivity of your intimacy. Prayerfully consider if there are any relationships that must be severed in order to cherish the exclusivity that the Lord demands in your marriage.
5. Spend time in prayer asking God to help you serve your spouse, love your spouse, and pray for your spouse.

A Prayer for You

"Father, we thank you for bringing us together. You fashioned the two of us that we might partner together in the task of bringing you glory. Thank you for complementing our strengths and weaknesses so brilliantly. Thank you for the love that we enjoy on a daily basis. Thank you that we are not alone.

"We confess the ways in which we have not been exclusive in our thoughts and actions toward each other. Forgive us for allowing other people and situations to crowd out our pure devotion to each other. In whatever way our hearts may have strayed from each other, we ask for your forgiveness. We confess whatever lustful thoughts we may have entertained about others. Forgive us for not cherishing each other in the ways that you expect. We know that the occasional indifference toward each other is symptomatic of the greater issue of our cold hearts toward you. Turn our eyes back to each other that our marriage might reflect the purity of love you have for your church.

"We thank you for sending Jesus to die on the cross for our sins that we might live free from the bondage of these sins. Thank you for the power of the resurrection and the life and victory it brings us in our marriage. Teach us to walk in this victory.

"Help each of us to be quick to confess the ways in which our hearts wander. Grant us humble hearts that understand how our wandering devastates each other and weakens our marriage. Help us to avoid situations where we will be overcome by temptation. Give us hearts that long to be devoted to each other. In Jesus' name, Amen."

Chapter 3

SEX IS UNIFYING

Scripture Reading: Song of Solomon 3

Even on your worst days, sex can drive you toward your spouse in ways that defy comprehension. How is it that you can desire your spouse so strongly even when you are frustrated with them? How do you explain a sexual attraction that overpowers your irritation with your spouse? Your need to express yourself sexually with your spouse is stronger than your need to win arguments or have your way in the relationship. Sex can soften your heart and bring you closer to your spouse when other attempts haven't worked. The vulnerability required in sex helps husbands and wives communicate with each other. In a world filled with mounting pressures, sex catapults your marriage to the very top of your priority list. Even when the world spirals out of control, your desire to ravish your wife is not affected in the least. Sex can make you rush home from work to be with your spouse. Sex can encourage you to take that desperately needed romantic vacation with your spouse. God uses sex to unify your marriage.

After the Lord created Eve and brought her to Adam, the Scripture says, "That is why a man leaves his father and mother and is united to his wife, and they become one flesh" (Gen. 2:24). Jesus affirmed this incredible reality in Matthew 19:6, saying, "So they are no longer two, but one flesh. Therefore, what God has joined together, let man not separate." Think about that for a moment. God does not simply want you and your spouse to be close. He is aiming for one flesh. Becoming one flesh enables you to work more effectively in your service to the Lord.

Remember, God made woman so that Adam would have a suitable "helper" (Gen. 2:18). You will not labor effectively for Christ if your marriage is fractured and full of discord.

In my own life, I constantly need Stephanie's discernment, support, and prayers. Especially when it comes to critical decision points, Stephanie's voice gives me perspective and clarity. Her words and suggestions help me make good decisions. Having a strong and unified marriage helps me be a good pastor. Any discord or rancor would eventually erode my credibility as the undershepherd of my church.

God gave us the wonderful gift of sexual intimacy, in part, to foster the "one flesh" principle in marriages. As Dr. Lehman notes, "a fulfilling sex life is one of the most powerful marital glues a couple can have."[1] Sexual intimacy promotes unity in marriage, which, in turn, promotes more effective work for the cause of Christ. This is one of the reasons why this book is so important. It's not just about achieving great sex. Great lovers will have successful marriages and be more effective for the cause of Christ.

I'm constantly amazed at how difficult serving the Lord can be. It takes an incredible amount of stamina, resolve, and faith. You have to have an unflinching commitment to serving Christ amidst difficult circumstances. Without question, this requires an incredible measure of cooperation with your spouse. Effective cooperation is inseparable from the task of being able to understand and anticipate the needs of your partner. If you do not understand your spouse when it comes to such a fundamental aspect of who they are, how in the world could

---

1. Kevin Leman, *Sheet Music: Uncovering the Secrets of Sexual Intimacy in Marriage* (Carol Stream, IL: Tyndale, 2008), 45.

you partner effectively with them? If you and your spouse are not on the same page when it comes to this fundamental aspect of your humanity, then it's hard to imagine how you could ever experience optimal cooperation when it comes to serving the Lord. So we need to ask the question, "How can we maximize the unity and cooperation so that we can be more effective for the cause of Christ?" I can assure you that at least part of the answer is to not ignore each other's physical needs.

Is it even possible to have unity amidst an unhealthy sexual relationship? How could you lie coldly beside your spouse in bed, ignore their physical needs, and then expect to have a close marriage? How many nights of this would it take for a deep resentment to quell the unity of your marriage? It would be naïve to expect open and honest communication while denying your spouse the needs that God designed them to have. Would you even want to be unified with a person who seems satisfied in leaving you so unsatisfied? So whereas some might dismiss Song of Solomon as somehow unspiritual and carnal, we see now how incredibly important it is.

Sex Works like a Magnet

The palpable desire to express their love physically acts like a magnet, one that drives the lovers in Song of Solomon toward each other over and over. The drive that they have for each other is especially clear when they are apart. She compares her husband to a gazelle: "Here he comes, leaping across the mountains, bounding over the hills. My beloved is like a gazelle or a young stag . . ." (2:8–9). His longing to be with her drove him like a gazelle that can run at speeds of up to sixty mph. And when they are together, their love intimately keeps them up all night, "Until the day breaks and the shadows flee" they intoxicate each other with love (2:17; 4:6). And during the day, they nestle themselves underneath the cover of trees (1:16–17) and in the vineyards (7:11–13) to make love. They are not forcing themselves to hang out or having to schedule appointments to make sure that they don't forget to spend time together. They are irresistibly drawn to each other. . . just like magnets.

Some magnets require over a thousand pounds of force to pull them apart. I think the lovers in Song of Solomon would require an even greater force to pull them apart. She says, “I held him and would not let him go till I had brought him to my mother’s house, to the room of the one who conceived me” (3:4). The Hebrew verb translated “I held him . . .” is a very strong word used in context with battle. She grabs her husband with the same force that a soldier might seize his enemy and takes him to the room where she can make love to him. What else can drive somebody toward their spouse in this manner?

The reverse can also be true. Have you ever turned magnets over and felt them repel each other? If you are not meeting each other’s needs, the issue of sex drives you away from each other. Learning and growing in this area of your marriage will guard you from fighting over this precious gift that God has given you.

Sex Strengthens

Making love to your spouse can strengthen your marriage in ways that nothing else can. Perhaps you have known couples who live in constant strife. If they have been open with you about their issues, there is a good chance you have picked up that they also struggle in the area of sexual intimacy. It’s not just that they are not on the same page or that they struggle to communicate. An impenetrable wall can form in marriages where there is limited or, in some cases, no healthy sexual intimacy. I think you will find that the opposite is also true. With couples who enjoy the fullness of what God intended sexual intimacy to be, there is glorious unity. While there will always be challenges in communication and moments when our selfishness gets the best of us, unity can flourish when sexual intimacy does.

Over the course of your marriage, you will face many pressures that threaten the health of your relationship. Have you ever argued with your spouse over your family’s finances? Do your personal struggles with sin create tension in your marriage? Have you felt the daily pressures of your job drive a wedge between the two of you?

If so, you are not alone. Not only do we face the normal pressures of life that distract us from the person that God has placed in our life, but Satan, who prowls like a lion, actively searches for ways to destroy your marriage. God knew that you would need something to drive you relentlessly toward your spouse. When the challenges of life threaten to push us away, the desire to express our love for our spouse drives us to be as close as we can. God knew that sexual intimacy in your marriage would foster openness and communication. He knew that it would help you crave your spouse's presence. God protects the unity of your marriage as you love your spouse sexually.

Sex Prioritizes the Marriage Relationship

If you are not careful, your friendships with others will become more important to you than your marriage relationship. Without the gift of sexual intimacy, your marriage relationship would not be that much different from other relationships. The only difference would be that you live underneath the same roof. A spouse should be so much more than a roommate. The gift of sexual intimacy distinguishes the marriage relationship as distinct from every other. Your spouse is the only person on the planet that you enjoy this special gift with. Your wife is not just your sidekick or your buddy. And your husband is not just the guy you keep around to maintain the lawn and occasionally lift heavy things. Sexual intimacy signifies that your spouse is your lover.

Without sexual intimacy, you might also be tempted not to give your spouse the time and attention that they need. Men especially would fight the temptation to become extremely lackadaisical and careless toward their spouse. In fact, in marriages that neglect sexual intimacy, this is precisely how they might treat each other. I do not detect even a hint of indifference between the lovers in the Song of Solomon. They treat each other as though they are the most important people in the cosmos. Sexual intimacy gives them the ideal way to express their powerful affections toward each other. It creates a laser-like focus on each other that stokes the flames of their mutual love and adoration.

If Sex Is Unifying, Why Do We Argue about It?

How could a gift that is designed to promote unity in a marriage be the subject of so much consternation? If you have ever argued about sex in your marriage, don't panic: that makes you normal. Even in the greatest marriages, there are occasional spats over sex. Here are a few of the greatest contributing factors.

We Have Different Needs

God made you different from your spouse. You are different, not only by virtue of your gender but also as a result of your personality. That's okay. In many cases, these differences promote compatibility in marriages. However, sometimes our needs collide when we put ourselves first and don't pay enough attention to what our spouse needs. As we will talk about in chapter 8, you don't have to choose whose needs get met in a marriage. Learn to put your spouse first and trust that God will give them the grace to also meet your needs.

We Change

You and your spouse will go through seasons of change. There is a reason that most of us don't like change. Change is hard. Throughout your marriage, you will experience changes that affect your sex life. A significant change in your job can drastically affect your stress level and therefore your desire for intimacy. The stress of new expectations at your job could keep your mind so occupied that you think less about sex, or it could render you unusually desperate for a sexual release. At a minimum, longer hours will change the rhythm of when you make love, and therefore, the frequency. Your health can also drastically affect your sex life. If you do not feel well, there is a 100 percent chance that your desire for sex will decrease. Necessary changes in medication can also negatively affect your desire for intimacy. Financial pressures can also leave you and your spouse needing very different things. When it comes to disrupting the rhythm of your sex life, you can be sure that having your first child will do the job. Waiting to make love until after the six-week checkup will be the least of your worries post baby. During these seasons of change, you will have to pray and navigate through how these changes negatively affect intimacy. In order to do this, you must communicate.

We Don't Communicate

It's hard to meet your spouse's needs when you don't know what they are. As with so many other arguments in marriage, a lack of communication is often to blame for arguments about sex. If you don't communicate about intimacy, you are destined to argue about it. The good news is that so many of the problems are avoidable if you simply know what is going on with your spouse. Are you and your spouse able to talk openly about sex? If you are not, you may find that the subject only comes up when you argue about it. Don't blame your spouse for not meeting expectations that you have never communicated.

We Have Unreasonable Expectations

Your spouse was not created for the sole purpose of bringing you sexual fulfillment. Your spouse will not be able to meet all your expectations all of the time. It simply will not happen. Even if all your expectations are reasonable, you are married to an imperfect person. If you react sharply to every unmet expectation, you will find yourself arguing about sex a whole lot. God wants to sanctify you through your marriage. He longs for the partnership of your marriage to strengthen your impact on those around you. If you are not able to always meet your spouse's expectations, this makes your marriage normal. The challenge for every Christian is to find your ultimate contentment in Christ and not in what your spouse is able to do for you in the bedroom.

Unity with Christ

The unity between a husband and wife should symbolize the unity between Christ and His church (Eph. 5:31–32). For those who have become God's children through faith in Jesus Christ, sex foreshadows the future glories of union with Christ.[2] One day, the church will be

---

2. Timothy Keller, *The Meaning of Marriage: Facing the Complexities of Commitment with the Wisdom of God* (New York: Riverhead Books, 2011), 271.

presented to Christ as a pure virgin (2 Cor. 11:2). The apostle John writes, "Let us rejoice and be glad and give him glory! For the wedding of the Lamb has come, and his bride has made herself ready" (Rev. 19:7). Having been joined to Christ, believers will spend eternity in a sublime place called heaven. Sex is "the most ecstatic, breathtaking, daring, scarcely-to-be-imagined look at the glory that is our future."[3] The unspeakable joys of sexual intimacy in marriage don't even come close to the supreme joy of eternal union with Christ in heaven!

Unified Marriages, Unified Churches

Thousands of churches close their doors each year. What a tragedy that churches entrusted with the responsibility of shining the light of Christ are growing dim all across America. We can't plant enough churches to replace the ones that are closing their doors every year. An alarming number of churches that are planted to fill the void face the same fate in a matter of years. Many of these churches died because they failed to experience the unity that the New Testament admonishes us to have. Selfish squabbles and petty agendas through generations have driven people from the one institution that should epitomize unity.

How can churches unite in mission and fellowship if they are filled with people who have failed to experience peace in their homes? Those conditioned to interact selfishly in their marriages will eventually act the same way with their brothers and sisters in Christ, creating a toxic environment that few will tolerate. Do you see how quickly your marriage can have a noxious influence on those for whom Christ died? On the other hand, a unified, strong marriage is a dynamic and powerful force. God can use strong marriages to defend the fellowship of the body of Christ. God wants to use your marriage to promote this glorious unity in your church. You have an obligation before God to cultivate peace and unity in your place of worship. Don't start by

3. Ibid.

pointing out the flaws of other church members. Instead, start with your own marriage. Leverage the wonderful gift of sexual intimacy to galvanize a strong marriage for the glory of God.

Homework

1. How has God promoted unity in your marriage through sexual intimacy?
2. What changes in life are affecting your sex life? What are some ways that you can adjust your intimacy through this season of change?
3. Complete the following sentence: "When it comes to sex, I've always wanted to ask you about . . ."
4. What kind of impact does your marriage have on the body of Christ?

A Prayer for You

"Father, thank you for uniting us in marriage. We give you thanks for weaving our lives together so beautifully. You desire for our marriage to remain strong and unified. Father, forgive us for the ways in which we have compromised the strength of our bond.

"Help us not to approach our relationship as two independent persons. Keep us from interacting with each other in a spirit of rigid individualism. Help us to dream together, play together, worship together, and serve together. Teach us to think about each other instead of just ourselves. Convict us of any activity that hinders the unity of our marriage. Help us to hurt when our spouse hurts and to rejoice when our spouse rejoices. May we never take the strength of our marriage for granted. Instead, help us to strive toward greater unity.

"We pray that the gift of sexual intimacy will drive us passionately toward each other. Increase our sexual desire for each other so that the vows that we made before you remain resilient. Protect us from the kind of influences that might sabotage the unity of our marriage. May the unity of our marriage be a strong symbol of the bond that you have with your church. Use our marriage to bless other marriages. Help us to always set a positive example for our brothers and sisters in Christ.

"Make our marriage strong so that we can weather any storm of life. Keep us strong through every season of life. Shepherd our marriage through every disappointment, hardship, and pain. Leverage even the most difficult times in life to strengthen our marriage.

"What you have joined together, let no man separate. In Jesus' name, Amen."

Chapter 4

SEX IS THE HARVEST OF MUTUAL ADMIRATION

Scripture Reading: Song of Solomon 4

When it comes to loving your spouse well, there is a powerful weapon in your arsenal you are most likely not using to your full advantage. Admiration. Your powerful feelings of love and adoration for your spouse will not fully benefit your marriage until you communicate them. The most brilliant musicians will have zero impact on people until they play or sing their melodies where people can hear them. How does it benefit anybody to keep those magnificent melodies hidden where nobody can enjoy them? Don't make the mistake of thinking that you can enhance your sex life merely by improving your technique. A happening sex life is not about mastering techniques or positions. Instead, it is about the position of your heart toward your spouse.

Sexual intimacy improves as you learn to appreciate the person you married. When you were first married, you could wax eloquent on all of the things that you loved about your spouse. Those around you probably grew weary of hearing everything that you had to say. But over time, things change and you tend to focus on all of the things that don't seem quite right anymore. The idiosyncrasies that used to be cute and funny might bother you now. If you are serious about strengthening your sex life, it is time to start appreciating your spouse all over again.

The reality is that you are so blessed that God has given you a spouse who uniquely complements you as a person. You are blessed to have somebody to share life with. You are blessed to have a friend and companion who understands you. You are blessed in so many ways. It's time for you to start noticing all of the wonderful things about your spouse. Your love life will directly correspond with your ability to understand just how blessed you are. The more you take your spouse for granted, the more you will struggle in the area of sexual intimacy. As you learn to verbally admire and adore your spouse, you will begin to see a wonderful harvest in the area of sexual intimacy. One thing is clear, the lovers in Song of Solomon are definitely not holding back when it comes to adoring each other. Let's examine first how she has learned to admire her husband.

Respect Your Husband

I can remember our first fight as if it was yesterday. We were driving to Fort Worth, Texas, when Stephanie told me she still had her father's credit card. She explained that her dad liked her to keep a credit card in case of emergencies. My pride was wounded at the thought that she might not trust me to take care of her. So I objected, saying that it wouldn't be necessary now that we were married. She disagreed and said she wasn't in the mood to discuss it. I persisted until she finally said, "Fine, I'll give him the credit card. It's not a big deal."

Upon hearing her say this, my childish pride instantly deflated. After she expressed willingness to respect something that she didn't agree with, I instantly gave up whatever ground I thought I had won. I didn't care about the credit card in the least; I just needed to hear her say that she respected me as the leader of our home. Oh, what I would give for that credit card today! No, seriously, after years of marriage, I've matured, but my need to feel her respect has not changed in the least. Though I pray that I don't act as sophomoric as I did on that day, my need for respect is as strong as ever.

If you looked to the world for advice on improving your sex life, I sincerely doubt that you would hear anybody encourage you to respect your husband. What on earth does respect have to do with an incredible sex life? Wives, your husband's desire for respect is even greater than his desire for physical intimacy. As you look beneath the layers of erotic language in Song of Solomon, you will observe a profound level of respect that this woman has for her husband. Her husband needs this respect in order to show her the affection that she desires. She is doing exactly what the apostle Paul challenges every wife to do in Ephesians 5:33 in saying, "and the wife must respect her husband." Your respect for your husband has nothing to do with him being more valued in the eyes of God. Men and women are loved equally by God. Instead, it has to do with the role that God has given him as the leader of your marriage. Her respect for him is one of the primary factors driving them closer to each other.

Beginning in the very first chapter, she says, "Pleasing is the fragrance of your perfumes; your name is like perfume poured out. No wonder the young women love you!" (1:3). A good name in the Bible is something to be sought after. Proverbs 22:1 teaches, "A good name is more desirable than great riches; to be esteemed is better than silver or gold." A good name was considered to be more fragrant "than fine perfume" (Eccles. 7:1). And, of course, she is not just referring to what his parents named him. Instead, his name represents the culmination of who he is as a man. In other words, she is saying that her husband is such a great man that even the mention of his name is a fragrant thing. So fragrant that the "young women adore" him. In essence, she is saying, "I'm the most blessed woman in the world to call you my husband."

Her respect is even more evident in chapter 5. In a dream she faces his sudden disappearance and frantically searches everywhere for him. In her desperate pursuit, she runs into people who challenge her affection, saying, "How is your beloved better than others, most beautiful of women? How is your beloved better than others, that you so charge us?" (v. 9). She could have responded with irritation, saying, "I'm so mad at him, he never comes home on time . . . he's always late." She did not say, "I'm glad he's gone—he snores too loud." She did not assume the worst about him or accuse him of anything. Instead, she responds in a manner that demonstrates her profound respect for her husband. With a battery of compliments, she lavishes respect on her husband, saying,

> My beloved is radiant and ruddy, outstanding among ten thousand. His head is purest gold; his hair is wavy and black as a raven. His eyes are like doves by the water streams, washed in milk, mounted like jewels. His cheeks are like beds of spice yielding perfume. His lips are like lilies dripping with myrrh. His arms are rods of gold set with topaz. His body is like polished ivory decorated with lapis lazuli. His legs are pillars of marble set on bases of pure gold. His appearance is like Lebanon, choice as its cedars. His mouth is sweetness itself; he is altogether lovely. (5:10–16)

She is not content to say something vanilla, like "I have a great man." She literally counts the ways, beginning with how exceptional he is. In her eyes, he is "ruddy" and "notable among ten thousand" (v. 10). Though not common to our vernacular, the word "ruddy" is significant because it is used to describe one of the mightiest men of the Old Testament, David (1 Sam. 16:12). If ten thousand men were lined up in front of her to choose from, she would pick her husband.

She also praises him for being powerful and strong, saying, "His body is like polished ivory" (v. 14). Though we don't commonly equate ivory with power, some of the most powerful beasts are associated with this description. Elephants, walruses, and whales all wield powerful tusks to hunt and protect their young. His strength is not a frightful brute force, but a power that has been beautifully sculpted like "marble" (v. 15). As marble is formed through countless years of pressure, so his legs represent the strength that comes from prevailing amidst the challenges of life. She also likens his strength to the cedars of Lebanon, which are broken only at the powerful force of God's mighty voice (Ps. 29:5).

As I contemplate these descriptions, I am reminded of how unlikely it is to receive this manner of praise from the world. Know this: the world will try very hard to beat your husband down. His coworkers will belittle his contributions and overlook his knowledge and expertise. In the competitive work arena, he may face scorn and ridicule. In the face of challenges and failures, your husband may feel as though he has let you and other family members down. Plagued by feelings of inadequacy, your husband may distance himself from you emotionally.

Even from childhood, boys are sizing themselves up by how they compare with others. Who is the strongest, the fastest, or the most talented? We never stop measuring our worth even in adulthood; the benchmarks just become more and more difficult to achieve. How much money we make a year, what our title at the office is, or the kind of house we can afford spark vexing comparisons in the minds of men. Most men can handle not feeling the respect from others in the world, but they will be utterly crushed if they think you feel the same way. Your heartfelt respect for your husband will mean more to him than the praise of ten thousand. In fact, if you are not among those cheering in the crowd, he can't even hear the crowd. Dozens of compliments on my sermons don't go near as far as a single nod from my wife. But truth be told, your husband will rarely have a crowd cheering him on. God has called you to champion your husband, to be his greatest cheerleader. Encourage him, support him, and lift him up in prayer so that he can be the husband you need.

The reality is this: it's so hard to be a great husband and father. He might not talk about it, but there are times when he's scared. Your husband needs your affirmation. Do you build your husband up or tear him down? Do you belittle him with taunting comments such as "He can't fix anything around the house," or "He can't clean worth a flip," or "He never follows through"? Do you roll your eyes at the mention of him? Does he hear you sarcastically teasing him from across the room? Even when these remarks are meant to amuse, they have a negative effect on a marriage. Proverbs 26:18–19 teaches, "Like a maniac shooting flaming arrows of death is one who deceives their neighbor and says, 'I was only joking!'" One need only read about the dangers of the tongue in James 3 to be sufficiently warned of the dangers of your words. In James' words, "the tongue also is a fire, a world of evil among the parts of the body. It corrupts the whole body, sets the whole course of one's life on fire, and is itself set on fire by hell" (James 3:6). In this context, our words remind me of mosquito bites. One bite is really not that big of a deal, but a swarm of bites can literally make you sick. Let's face it: things aren't really funny unless there is some basis of truth in them. The hint of truth in your mocking remarks will cause your husband to recoil from you.

If it's true that "love always protects," you would never want a derisive word about your husband to cross your lips (1 Cor. 13:7). The world will tear him up; it's your job to build him up. Don't nag him and become a "constant dripping" (Prov. 27:15). Instead, choose to be a source of strength, life, and affirmation for him! Now, I'm not saying you need to sugarcoat everything. There will be more than a few times in your marriage when you will need to speak the hard truths with love. But resolve that you will be the one person in his life who will love and respect him unconditionally. Don't bemoan what your husband is not; instead, start appreciating who he is and who God made him to be. Choose to focus on the areas where he excels far beyond other men. Your extraordinary love and respect will make him exceptional!

Respect Him around Others

What a wife says about her husband is significant, but who she says it to is equally important. She describes him to others, whereas he affirms her to her face. The need of respect for the bond of marriage is so significant. A husband will feel that respect when he knows that his wife speaks well of him in front of others. It is important that she praises him to his face, but notice the bulk of her praise is spoken in front of others. This makes him feel respect. The real test of your respect is how you talk about your husband when he is not around. How you talk to your neighbors, parents, and friends about your husband is even more important than what you say to his face. As it seems appropriate, let others know what you love about your husband.

What If You Find It Difficult to Respect Him?

Your husband will not always be the ideal husband, just as you will not always be the ideal wife. If you've been married for any length of time, you know this already. Just like you, your husband is downright imperfect. Your husband will sin and make mistakes. Life is sure to provide plenty of challenges that he may not always respond well to. Recognizing that you will not always respect everything he does and says, here are a few things to think about.

1. **Respect the Role He Plays in Your Marriage.** You can respect your husband as the leader of your marriage even if he is not always doing everything just right. God made him the leader of your home. God has called you to submit to him as unto the Lord. The apostle Paul says, "For the husband is the head of the wife as Christ is the head of the church" (Eph. 5:23). Disregarding the role that God has given him is tantamount to rejecting the leadership of Christ over his Church. Even when you can't respect something he has said or done, you can respect the role that God has given him to play in your marriage.
2. **Be Patient.** How do you want to be treated when you struggle to be the woman that God has called you to be? Sometimes you can learn something in days or weeks. But sometimes God sanctifies us over the course of months and years. Know there are things in your own life that you are struggling with. Knowing how patient God has been with you, why would you demand or require that your husband learn something overnight? God is Lord over the sanctification process, not you, and He will cause your husband to grow and change in His timing.
3. **Pray.** The most powerful weapon in your arsenal when it comes to helping your husband become the man God has called him to be is prayer. Though you may be tempted to correct, scold, and

shame your husband, God is calling you to pray. You will accomplish more through prayer than you can through criticizing him. Your prayers are more powerful than ten thousand words spoken out of irritation and contempt. Move your husband by spending time on your knees in prayer.

4. **Love Him for Who He Longs to Be.** On his worst day, love your husband for the man he longs to be for you. If your husband loves the Lord, he will feel a greater sense of failure than whatever shame you think you could lay on him. Don't punish him because he's having a hard time being the kind of example that we see in this book. If you deny him sexual intimacy because he's having a difficult time, he will deny you of your needs when you are having a difficult time. Give him what he needs even though he's not yet where he needs to be. Take care of him and he will work hard to take care of you.
5. **Your Job Is Not to Train Him or Fix Him.** You are powerless to change even the smallest things, such as how he squeezes the toothpaste. What makes you think you could change the far more significant aspects of his character? No amount of lecturing or complaining will change even the slightest thing about your husband. The one thing that it can accomplish for certain is driving your husband further from you in resentment. Your job is to love him for who he aspires to be. If you want him to continue to strive toward being the man that you need him to be, you should encourage him along the way. Don't withhold intimacy from him when he's not at his best. Encourage him, even in failure, when you know that his heart is longing in the right direction. Be patient with him and love him to the point where he can emulate the example of Song of Solomon.

Do you want to be adored and pursued by your husband, like the wife in Song of Solomon? If you long to experience a husband who will leap over mountains to pursue you, then cultivate respect for him in your marriage. Do you want a husband who will cherish you like the husband in Song of Solomon? Do you want a man who will lavish you with compliments? Do you want to see him desire you like the husband in Song of Solomon? If so, cultivate a godly respect for your husband.

It will be difficult for your husband to feel your respect if he thinks that his sexual needs are not important to you. If his needs are belittled or ignored, it will be hard for him to see respect from you. Imagine if he scoffed at the idea of listening to you share your thoughts and feelings. When you respect his strong sexual desire for you, he hears you saying, "You matter to me," "You are important to me," "You are a good husband." Sex can communicate these things in a way that nothing else can. Absent sex, your words might fall on deaf ears.

Your respect for your husband will accomplish more for your marriage than you can possibly comprehend. Here is the incredible thing, "When a woman nourishes, nurtures, and affirms her spouse, her love for him deepens."[1] A holy respect for your husband will heat up your love life as almost nothing else can.

Having looked at the example that God gives wives, it's now time to turn our attention to what He expects of husbands.

Adore Your Wife

Your job is to make your wife feel like the most adored woman in the world! "But," you might say, "I do adore my wife, so why am I not having the kind of passion Song of Solomon describes?" Let's be clear, we are not talking about merely thinking or feeling a certain way about your wife. Your wife needs to hear you adore her! That's right, you may actually have to open your mouth and speak. Don't panic, you can do this! She has a fundamental need to feel attractive in your eyes. Whereas you prefer visual stimuli, your wife is far more auditory. This means that you will need to audibly communicate your affection for

---

1. Bryan Chapell, *Each for the Other* (Grand Rapids: Baker Books, 2005), 113.

her. I say "audibly" because men can be terribly nonverbal . . . myself included. It's so easy to assume that your wife knows how you think and feel about her. But there is a good chance that she either doesn't know or doubts how you feel. Even if she does know it, that doesn't mean she doesn't need to hear it. Your wife's natural insecurities create a need for you to reassure her in your relationship. Don't ever let your wife wonder if you still find her attractive. Don't think for a moment that your wife hasn't worried about this. The wife in Song of Solomon definitely struggled with this.

She says, "Daughters of Jerusalem, I am dark like the tents of Kedar, yet lovely like the curtains of Solomon. Do not stare at me because I am dark, for the sun has gazed on me. My mother's sons were angry with me; they made me a keeper of the vineyards. I have not kept my own vineyard" (1:5–6). Having dark skin was not something to be desired in the ancient world, so she feels unattractive. She's basically saying, "I don't feel pretty because we were poor and I had to work outside." And to make matters worse, "My family was dysfunctional and my brothers treated me with disrespect." Like many women today, she feels ordinary. She compares herself to what was likely a very common flower, saying, "I am a rose of Sharon, a lily of the valleys" (2:1). She does not feel exceptional or beautiful.

If your wife feels this way, then you have much work to do in affirming her.

It is difficult for your wife to engage sexually with you if she does not feel attractive. Husbands, remember your wife is inundated every day of her life with not so subtle messages that there is only one acceptable body type. Through magazines, television, and every form of advertising, she compares herself to the one arbitrary figure that is both unnatural and unattainable for the majority of women. The multibillion-dollar cosmetic industry daily exploits the insecurities of women who long to be beautiful in their husbands' eyes, to say nothing of the Evil One who works relentlessly to make her feel worthless. Remember, the Devil is a slanderer and the Father of Lies (John 8:44). Don't think for a moment that he has not whispered things such as "You are too fat," "You are too thin," "You are too wrinkled," "You are too short," "Your skin is too pale," or "Your husband doesn't even find you attractive anymore." Do you think it beyond Satan to line up another man who will say all the things that you fail to say?

Before you and your wife were married, you keenly appreciated everything about her—maybe even to the exclusion of recognizing her weaknesses. You relished opportunities to sneak glances at her beauty. You would talk on the phone for hours, telling her over and over how much you adored her. Perhaps you flirted back and forth on the phone through text messages. After you are married, however, the reverse often happens. It's easy to focus on the things that are not ideal from your perspective and forget all the things that drew you to her in the first place. Don't take her inner and outer beauty for granted.

Men, a compliment is a powerful weapon in your arsenal when it comes to cultivating intimacy with your spouse. I want you to think about your words not as empty verbal gestures, but as powerful tools that lift your wife's desire for you to new heights. Think of a heartfelt compliment like a car jack. It does not look like much, but it can accomplish something your muscles can't. Beautiful words spoken from your heart can do so much to strengthen the sexual intimacy of your marriage. Her desire for you has nothing to do with how much money you make or what kind of reputation you've earned in the community. Your physical appearance is not the driving force behind her desire for you.

She just wants to be treasured by you. Verbally adoring your wife is like preheating the oven to 350 degrees. If you hope to get to broil, you need to warm her up. Please don't mishear what I'm saying. It's not about using words to manipulate your wife's desire for you. If that's your motivation, then I promise you it won't work, because she will see right through it. Women are far more discerning than you ever dreamt of being.

Your wife needs to *hear* you affirm her. Before you give your compliment, make sure that it is complimentary. But before we talk about how to do this, let's take a look at what not to do. Perish the thought of ever sounding like this guy . . .

> Honey, you still look nice to me, almost as nice as you did on the day we married. You really are a pretty good wife. I know you think you're overweight, but I promise . . . you're really not *that* fat. Old is not a word I would ever use to describe you. When I see your face, I am reminded of how hard life has been. I know you're not perfect, but I am still rather fond of you most of the time. I've stopped wondering what life would've been like had I married the other woman. Seriously, I am pretty sure that I made the right decision. So even if I can't change those things that irritate me, I want you to know that I am thankful for you. After all, you wouldn't be you without all your quirks and imperfections. You are way better than average in most respects. I hope I die first so that I don't have to be alone.
>
> Signed,
> Your Loving Husband

Let's just say this cringeworthy sonnet will not give your wife butterflies or make her go weak in the knees. Only a self-indulged, calloused man could make his wife feel like a worn-out rag. I know you can do better than this. But if you can't . . . perhaps silence is the better option.

After my wife became pregnant with our first child, I made the terrible mistake of agreeing with her one day. Usually in marriage, agreeing with your wife is a smart thing to do, but not in this case. We were driving home one day when my wife was describing how she looked pregnant. It was early enough that she didn't actually look pregnant, but she definitely had put on a few pounds. She said, "I feel like I don't look pregnant yet. I just look like I've had too many donuts." I responded with the dreaded "Yeah." It was as though time stopped after I allowed that dreadful word to leave my lips. It was one thing for her to say it, but quite another for me to agree. Had I been a Jedi, I would've waved my hand over her face and said, "You did not hear anything." But a Jedi I was not.

Think Carefully

It's clear that the husband has thought carefully about his bride. He works hard to compare her to the most flattering images. Using word pictures that had profound meaning for her, he describes how beautiful she is. "You are as beautiful as Tirzah, my darling, as lovely as Jerusalem, as majestic as troops with banners" (6:4). She would have known that Tirzah and Jerusalem were the "greatest cities in the early monarchy."[2] Basically, he's saying that she represents the very best of the nation of Israel. Her beauty is so forceful and powerful that he tells her to look away.[3]

Do you choose your words carefully, or do you simply shoot from the hip? Do your compliments have more to do with you than with her? Have you bungled your words so badly that she now feels more insecure? I don't care who you are: every husband has room to grow in this area. I suppose I should have thought more carefully before comparing my wife to a jelly donut. I really like jelly donuts, so I thought she might appreciate my sentiment. Come to find out, my flattery was not so flattering. Apparently, she was not going for the jelly-donut look.

Think about how carefully you craft your words when you are at work. Consider how judicious you are when you respond to critical emails. In my line of work, I have to be very measured and thoughtful with everything I say. Is your wife deserving of any less care? Perhaps you should choose your words carefully, much like a painter thoughtfully selects colors for his palette. Or like a composer who searches desperately to find the most harmonious notes for his composition. You don't need to be a poet to speak lovingly to your wife. Your words matter. Your wife will not soon forget what you say. This reality can be a blessing or a curse in your marriage. Yes, you definitely need to think

---

2. Duane A. Garrett, *Proverbs, Ecclesiastes, Song of Songs, The New American Commentary* (Nashville: Broadman, 1993), 417.
3. Ibid.

about what you say. But if you don't say the right things in the right manner, then you may not be getting anywhere at all.

Think about How You Will Say It

I want you to craft not only what you say but also how you say it. A coarse delivery can scuttle your best attempts at flattery. Choose the right moment where you will have the best opportunity to connect with her. Lay aside the voice you use in the office or with the kids. She's not a pupil in your class or a colleague down the hall—she's your wife. Look her in the eyes and speak to her from your heart. It does not have to rhyme or be long and flowery, but it needs to be true and heartfelt. If you are at a loss for words, then you have some homework to do.

Start by studying your wife. You may well have to work at this, since there's a good chance that you are not the most observant person. If you've ever found yourself saying, "Honey, since when were you a redhead?" you may need to sharpen your focus. She wants you to notice the small things that she does to be attractive in your eyes. She wants you to notice that she's worked hard to stay in shape or that she bought a new outfit to look the best she can in your eyes. Do you notice the efforts that she went through to put a delicious meal on the table? Just as a coach works to understand his players or a scientist studies his experiments, you need to study your wife. If you don't really know your wife, your best attempts in the bedroom will fall far short of her desires. Listen to how keenly the husband adores his wife.

If you find yourself at a loss for words, you can always start where this husband in Song of Solomon began: "How beautiful you are, my darling! Oh, how beautiful!" (4:1). But don't pat yourself on the back unless you've counted the ways. In various times throughout your day or week, let your wife hear you verbalize your attraction. From top to bottom, the husband eloquently articulates just how beautiful she is in his eyes by starting with *hers*:

> Your eyes are doves (4:1).

Whereas most guys might coarsely skip to their favorite body part, the husband begins with her eyes. More than any other body part, the eyes communicate the essence of a person's countenance and character. In a person's eyes you can see, joy, life, excitement, love, and so many other human emotions. As he looks into her soul, he sees so much love. In his eyes she is a beautiful person, not just an object he's drawn to. Doves were not pesky birds that menaced; they were animals that had incredible utility in the ancient world. Noah used a dove to determine whether or not the flood had receded (Gen. 8:8). The dove was also an important part of the sacrificial system (Lev. 1:14). And draped on either side of her beautiful eyes, he draws attention to her hair:

> Your hair is like a flock of goats descending from the hills of Gilead (4:1).

When was the last time you complimented your wife's hair? Consider for a moment the herculean efforts your wife goes through on Sunday morning while you sit anxiously in the car, trying with every ounce of your being to not honk the horn. Think about the thousands of bottles of shampoo, conditioner, and other potions (utterly incomprehensible to most men) she has purchased through the years trying to look her best for you. And even after all of her efforts, she climbs into the car to find not your adoring approval, but a scowl that essentially says, "You are making me late again." But before you carelessly spout off that her head looks like an old goat (this might not have the intended effect), you might benefit from understanding the ancient symbolism of "goats descending."

The husband is not comparing his wife's hair with the coarse garment of a goat, but rather the visual impact of seeing a large flock of goats streaming down Mount Gilead from a distance. Gilead was a beautiful part of the Transjordan, nourished by the Jabbok River. Its location made it ideal for pasture and was associated with the enormous herds of Jacob in Genesis 31 as well as the massive flocks belonging to Reuben's descendants in Numbers 32. In the ancient world, flocks always meant money. And the fact that the goats are "descending" conveys that her thick and precious hair is lushly cascading down the sides of her head. Think of those shampoo commercials that show in slow motion the model's silky hair waving in perfect synchronism across the screen, and you will understand what he's trying to communicate. The creativity of his admiration heightens the intensity of his compliments. Moving down her face, he now turns his attention to her mouth:

> Your teeth are like a flock of sheep just shorn, coming up from the washing. Each has its twin; not one of them is alone. Your lips are like a scarlet ribbon; your mouth is lovely. Your temples behind your veil are like the halves of a pomegranate (4:2–3).

Allow me to summarize. He loves her mouth, especially her lips and her teeth; not only are they clean, but she also isn't missing any of them. In our age of "highly sophisticated dentistry and orthodontics," we might be tempted to overlook this compliment as "droll."[4] But a mouth filled with teeth was not to be taken for granted in the ancient world. He loves the delicate, delicious, and colorful symmetry of her beautiful face. Her face is so delectable that he wants to taste her as he would a pomegranate. As a pomegranate is bursting with flavor, so his wife is equally luscious and delectable to him. As his eyes gaze lower, he cannot help but comment on her stately neck:

> Your neck is like the tower of David, built with courses of stone; on it hang a thousand shields, all of them shields of warriors (4:4).

The Tower of David was a provocative image that communicated royalty, strength, security, and dignity. It was the kind of image that everybody was familiar with. It demanded attention and honor. Much like the royal landmark of David's tower, her neck was worthy of adornment. This husband earnestly believes that his wife's neck

---

4. Duane A. Garrett and Paul R. House, *Song of Songs/Lamentations,* Word Biblical Commentary, Book 23 (Nashville: Thomas Nelson, 2004), 189.

is just as stately and majestic. When was the last time you adorned your wife's neck in a manner that communicated to her your attraction?

> Your breasts are like two fawns, like twin fawns of a gazelle that browse among the lilies (4:5).

I wish I could unpack the richness of this metaphor, but, unfortunately, the imagery is not entirely clear. But even without understanding the nuance, I think we can safely conclude that he really loves her breasts. He repeats his great affection for her breasts four times in Song of Solomon. God wants you to be satisfied with your wife's breasts (Prov. 5:19) and to communicate your attraction to her. Notice, he admires her breasts within the context of admiring so many other things about her. Every husband would be wise to follow suit. The husband moves beyond what she looks like and in verse 11 describes what she tastes like:

> Your lips drop sweetness as the honeycomb, my bride; milk and honey are under your tongue (4:11).

Of all of the senses, taste is definitely the most intimate. Though we are born wanting to put things in our mouths, over time we learn to be very discriminating about what we allow in our mouths. Before you devour some new exotic flavor, it's common to sample only the smallest amount possible. And if we find something objectionable, we don't think twice about spitting it out. The husband in Song of Solomon has found something more delectable than the sweetest of tastes—his wife's mouth. The power of his imagery leaves no question in her mind—he will not be content to merely taste the goodness of her mouth. As one may whet their appetite with a tasty hors d'oeuvre, he is ready to indulge in the main course. At this point, you would think that the husband would have exhausted all of his compliments, but not so! Now, he's ready to talk about what she smells like:

> Your plants are an orchard of pomegranates with choice fruits, with henna and nard, nard and saffron, calamus and cinnamon,

with every kind of incense tree, with myrrh and aloes and all the finest spices (4:13–14).

Fragrances are important to an overall experience. A beautiful aroma enhances wonderful experiences. Nobody wants to go to a restaurant, park, or store that smells bad. Smells repel us—or draw us in. One day, Stephanie and I were spending time in a beautiful garden when we were overwhelmed with the most glorious fragrance. It wasn't enough to simply enjoy the scent, we had to find the source and drink it in. The smell worked like a gravitational force. It lured us in until we stood right in front of it to take in all of its wonder. In the very same manner, the husband in Song of Solomon describes the fragrances that draw him closer to his wife. He could no more ignore the scent of his lover than he could a wonderful aroma of a rose.

All of Her

This husband has learned the art of appreciating everything about his wife. He did not speak only of her sexual organs or the body parts that enticed him the most. In fact, from his description, you wouldn't even know where his eyes gravitate the most. He gives roughly the same attention to her hair, neck, and teeth as he does her breasts. His gushing compliments help her feel more attractive. His comprehensive and thorough enjoyment of all that she is prepares her to give herself entirely to him. How could she withhold the things that he spent so much time adoring? In the same way, I think that his careful appreciation for her entire physical composition has cultivated a greater appetite for her. It's clear that their love life has not diminished into merely a sexual release for him that lasts only the span of a few minutes. No, he has work to do in enjoying all that she is. It's no wonder that it takes him all night (2:17). I don't think it's a coincidence that she offers him everything that he has so painstakingly admired.

Total Perfection

Was she really perfect? Are we to imagine that this young woman resembled the sort of airbrushed super-model seen on the cover of magazines? Not at all! But in the eyes of her husband, she was flawless. Though she is far from being physically perfect, he calls her "my flawless one" (5:2) and treats her as though she is the only woman who matters in the entire world. His eyes are so fastened upon her that she has become the standard by which every other woman is measured. As he looks at her, every other woman falls short. In his eyes, there is no other woman like her. She is not one among many that he could have spent the rest of his life with. Instead, she is the only one he wants. What's more, he has made it clear to her that she is the only one for him.

There is no woman in the world like your spouse. No one looks just like her. No one acts just like her or talks just like her. No one laughs just like her or smells just like her. There is not a single other woman on the planet who has her personality with all her idiosyncrasies. No other woman treats you in the way that she does. No other woman loves you as she does. No other woman has supported you as your wife has. No other woman has stood by your side as she has. No other woman has prayed for you as she has. Your wife is one of a kind. When was the last time you counted the ways?

The Work of a Master

> Your graceful legs are like jewels, the work of an artist's hands (7:1).

Your wife represents divine intentionality. God made your wife. Your wife represents the handiwork of a masterful Creator, who, in His infinite knowledge and wisdom, crafted her with you in mind. What an incredible thought! God was thinking of you when He made your spouse. There is nothing random when it comes to the physical characteristics of your spouse. As a masterful creation from God, she deserves the utmost love and care. The act of appreciating your wife should result in you drawing nearer to the God who created her!

Did It Work?

Lavishing these compliments appears to have a profound impact on her self-esteem. In chapter 1 you can hear her insecurities, "Dark am I . . . like the tents of Kedar" (1:5). But toward the end of the book I hear more confidence, "I am a wall and my breasts are like towers" (8:10). She does not appear the least bit inhibited and repeatedly invites her husband to make love to her. When she says, "I am like an unexceptional flower," he responds, "Like a lily among thorns is my darling among the young women" (2:1–2). To say she responded positively is a massive understatement. She responds, saying, "Like an apple tree among the trees of the forest is my beloved among the young men. I delight to sit in his shade, and his fruit is sweet to my taste" (2:3). Over and over she longs to give herself to the man whose eyes are fixed squarely upon her in the most loving way. In no uncertain terms, his verbal affirmation drives her desire to make love to him.

If you study your wife, you will identify hidden treasures only you would notice. Sharing your delight in these small gifts will go further than you can possibly know. When I was first married, there was no way I could have imagined the kind of wonderful mother Stephanie would become. The amount of work needed to keep our house running with four children is immense. Though I try to do what I can, Stephanie bears the weight of much of the daily housework. Stephanie does thousands of loads of laundry and has a constant flow of dirty dishes to contend with. And with four beautiful children come countless messes to clean up every day. Her hands become raw at times from washing them over and over. One day I was holding her hand, and I casually mentioned that her hands reminded me of the Proverbs 31 woman. The Proverbs 31 woman works with "eager hands" to provide for her family in so many ways (Prov. 31:13). To me, Stephanie's hands represent a life of loving her family well. This means so much more to me than her having polished gentile hands that never see a hard day's work. I was not prepared for the reaction that she gave. To my surprise, my comment meant the world to her, more than any overtly sexual comment could muster. Waxing eloquent about her physical characteristics could not have produced the same impact. Maybe you don't compliment her teeth or her hands, but surely there is some aspect of your wife's beauty that you have failed to highlight. In your quest to convey your attraction, don't overlook her inner beauty.

Admittedly, verbally affirming your wife is going to be hard for some of you. At first, it might feel awkward or uncomfortable. Chances are you are not accustomed to talking about how your wife makes you feel. You might even be a little bit nervous at how she will respond. Indeed, if she's not used to hearing you compliment her, she might act slightly puzzled at first. She might retort, "Who are you and what have you done with my husband?" But in her heart she will cherish your words. If I've learned anything about women, I've learned that they do not soon forget the words that come out of your mouth. This is true for better and for worse. Whatever the cost, you can be sure that the investment will reap a powerful return.

What are you saying to your wife to make her feel beautiful and willing to give herself to you? Make her feel like she is the only woman in the world. Don't allow a day to go by without verbally affirming her. You cannot stand to miss out on the blessing of verbally adoring the woman that God gave you. The next time her beauty creates an insatiable desire to make love to her, stop and do your best to put your attraction into words. Write your thoughts down on paper and leave her a note. Spend time thinking of all the things that you love about her, and watch your attraction for her grow. Your thoughtful, adoring words will go further than you can possibly imagine! But you also need to have reasonable expectations.

Don't assume that you will enjoy an erotic evening of lovemaking just because you managed to say a few nice things throughout the day. Your wife may be more likely to allow your words to marinate in her mind for a couple of days. At this point, you might feel frustrated and give up on affirming your wife. But don't stop. Build the habit of speaking life-giving words to your wife on a daily basis. Over time these words will bear a bountiful harvest if you continue to sow them.

Look Forward to the Harvest

God designed the covenant of marriage to be a safe, affirming environment where love and sexual intimacy can flourish. The respect and affirmation that you give each other will yield a tremendous harvest. An abundant harvest always makes the plowing and sowing worthwhile. In this case, the harvest will be a wonderful sexual enjoyment of each other. Joy will flood your marriage as you learn to treasure each other. The splendor of this harvest will make you strong against the temptations of this world. It will also prompt gratitude in your heart toward God. Through the process of adoring your spouse, you will learn how just how blessed you are. Don't miss out on the harvest. Adore your spouse!

Homework

Finish the following sentences to your spouse:

1. "I know you love and appreciate me when you say . . ."
2. "I've never told you how beautiful your . . ."
3. "I feel your respect when you . . ."
4. "I respect the way you . . ."
5. "I feel sexy and attractive when I hear you say . . ."
6. "You look most attractive to me when you . . ."
7. Write your wife a love note over the next week.

A Prayer for You

"Father, you know us so completely. You know our going and our coming. You are familiar with all our ways. Before a word is on our tongue, you know it completely. You knit each of us together in our mothers' wombs. You knew exactly what we needed in a spouse. Thank you for bringing us the ideal complement for how you have made us.

"Forgive us for all of the ways we have failed to communicate our admiration and respect for each other. Forgive us for the times when we diminished each other through our words or actions. We confess that we have not always showed the respect and admiration that you have called us to give to each other. Forgive us for every selfish and petty interaction we've had toward each other.

"Help us, Father, to see our differences as a means of you strengthening and sanctifying us in our areas of weakness. Help us to adore the differences in each other. In every case where we might be tempted to find fault with each other, help us to see the beauty in how you have made us. Give us grace to realize when we are at fault, when our natural inclinations do not reflect your righteousness. Teach us to be patient with each other while acknowledging that you are sovereign over our sanctification. Give us strength to trust you for our progress as individuals. Guard us from the sin of pride that makes us blind to the ways in which we need to change for the sake of our spouse.

"Bless our marriage as we learn to respect and adore each other. In every case where we might otherwise be tempted to respond sinfully, strengthen us to give grace. Give us a fresh awareness of how special you have made our spouse. Enable us to treasure each other. Help us to see their idiosyncrasies as evidence of your love for us. Help us to sacrificially serve each other in ways that strengthen our marriage. Strengthen our marriage as we learn to communicate our affection in ways that build each other up. In Jesus' name, Amen."

Chapter 5

SEX IS LOVE EXPRESSED

Scripture Reading: Song of Solomon 5

"Love is cleaning up throw-up." Yes, Mom was right, love does occasionally mean cleaning up throw-up, but thankfully that's not all it is. Love between a husband and wife can also mean a sensational sex life. The foundation for their white-hot passion for each other is love. Love is the fuel behind their sexual intimacy.

A God-glorifying sex life is the physical expression of a mighty love between a husband and wife. If you want your sexual relationship with your spouse to flourish, you must get back to the basics. You cannot separate a wonderful sex life from the far more foundational issue of love. If you do, all that remains is to discuss technique. But the primary focus of Song of Solomon is certainly not technique. There is no possibility of technique producing the kind of powerful relationship that these lovers enjoy. Yet, on cover after cover of trendy magazines, next to the photoshopped image of some beautiful person, it seems there is always an article promising some new technique for great sex. Sex is a physical expression of a strong love. Cultivate a stronger love for your spouse and your sex life will grow exponentially.

So let's talk about love.

How strong is your love for your spouse? This may seem like an odd question. We are not accustomed to thinking of love in these terms. It seems to many that you either love or you don't love. But that's not true. Love is always a question of degree. Not all love is created equal.

Remember what it was like in high school when you "fell in love" with that really cute guy or that beautiful girl in English class. Maybe you started dating or even thought that you would spend the rest of your life together. Compare the love you felt with the love between a couple who has been married for over sixty years. There is no comparison. The love between a couple that has been married for many years is so much stronger and deeper. One thing is clear; these lovers in Song of Solomon have an unbelievably strong love for each other. It's their love that drives their sexual relationship.

A Soul Love

We see a glimpse of her love for her husband in the way she refers to him. To her, he is not just the man she married or the one she is stuck with. He's not just the man who provides a roof over her head or the one who disappoints her. Over and over, she refers to him in this book as the one whom her "heart loves" (1:7; 3:1–4; 5:6). Literally in Hebrew, she describes him as the one her "soul loves." She loves him with the very essence of her being. She loves him with her entire life. Consequently, intimacy for her is not simply a means of pacifying the overactive sex drive of the man she lives with, but an act of love for the one her soul longs for. Does your soul long for your spouse? Wonderful sex will follow a soul love for your spouse.

Love Consumes

Holy love that exists between a husband and wife is a gloriously all-consuming force that benevolently overshadows you with an unshakeable, unquenchable desire for each other. You can feel this way about your spouse even when things are not going well in life. In Song of Solomon, chapter 3, the woman dreams that her husband has disappeared. Neither she nor the readers know where he is or why he is gone. Her response to his terrifying absence reveals the strength of her love for her husband. She says, "All night long on my bed I looked for the one my heart loves; I looked for him but did not find him" (3:1). She does not say, "Good, he's gone, he snores anyway," or, "Good, I will get to enjoy some me time." She does not launch into an angry diatribe about how he never calls when he's going to be late. She can't stand the thought of being away from her husband, especially since she does not know where he is and whether he is safe. In her dream she wrestles with his absence "all night long," waiting for him to return home. Marriage is the dissolving of two independent persons. We yearn with an all-consuming love for our spouse because God has joined us. Don't marry if you want to keep your life basically the same. Marriage is not friendship with benefits; it's a soul-consuming love for your spouse. Her consuming love for her spouse compels her to action.

Love Compels

Having waited all night for his return, she then takes action. Using three volitional Hebrew verb forms she conveys her determination to find him. Within the span of one short verse, she says, "I will get up," "I will go about the city," and "I will search" (3:2). She is not content to simply feel things toward her husband. Her love compels her to action. Love is by nature a compelling force. Your love for your spouse ought to compel you to do the kinds of things that you would not normally do. Does your love compel you to wash the dishes when you are tired or get up and cook breakfast when you are exhausted? Does your love compel you to lay down your interests for the well-being of your spouse? Love is a powerful force. It can empower you to do things that you never thought you were capable of. A compelling love causes intimacy in marriage to flourish.

Love Seals

She rouses her husband underneath the apricot tree and tells him, "Place me like a seal over your heart, like a seal on your arm" (8:6). What is a "seal"? This Hebrew word conveys something that is securely fastened. I think about Exodus 28, where the Lord tells Moses that

Aaron and his descendants are to wear sacred garments when they go into the most holy place. God wanted the names of the Sons of Israel to be fastened on these garments so that the priests would always be praying for the Israelites by name.[1] What a beautiful picture! She's saying, "Put me like a fixed seal on the most intimate place in your life, your heart." She's trying to tell him, "I want you to know in the core of your being that I am totally and completely yours, I belong to you, and you belong to me forever." She also wants this seal fixed on his arm so that everywhere he goes, people will know that he belongs to her and that she belongs to him. This is why most of us wear wedding rings: we want the world to know that we belong to somebody.

I want everybody to see the ring on Stephanie's finger. I want everybody to know that she is forever mine. I traveled to Riga, Latvia, several years ago on a mission trip. As we walked through the beautiful streets of downtown Riga, we came across a bridge covered in locks. Through the years, lovers had walked over this bridge, declared their love to each other, and fastened a lock on the bridge. What a beautiful way to begin a marriage . . . to say to the world that you have made a binding covenant, the kind that can no longer be undone.

The covenant that you have made with your spouse is more important than any other bond with a human being. The bond that you have with your spouse must be stronger than the bond you have with even your parents. It must be more secure than the bond you have with any of your friends or coworkers. It must be stronger than any other contractual agreement that you could ever enter into on this earth. You need to have the kind of secure bond that can never be compromised by the pressures of this life. The love you have for your spouse needs to be stronger than every disappointment, every pain, and every crisis you could ever experience.

But how can anyone be so certain about the strength of their rela-

1. Exod. 28:9–12.

tionship? If life is anything, it is unpredictable. Despite this reality, she knows that she will never walk away from him and that he will never leave her. How can she be so confident that she's not going to change her mind or decide that she wants another man? The answer to this is found in the very next description of her love.

Their Love Is Stronger than Death

Death, in the Hebrew mindset, was an uncontrollable force. Take Solomon, for example. He had accomplished so much in his life, yet he was completely powerless when it came to his death. He knew that there was positively nothing he could do about the fact that he would die just like the beasts of the field. We hear this same sentiment in Isaiah 5:14: "Therefore Death expands its jaws, opening wide its mouth; into it will descend their nobles and masses with all their brawlers and revelers." This verse personifies death as a being that opens its jaws and consumes the vile. Death is just as uncontrollable today as it was centuries ago. We cannot predict it, control it, or make it go away.

As one who has spent a lot of time around death, I promise you that people would do anything to prevent it. I will never forget the anguish in the eyes of one couple as they stared longingly at the tiny coffin holding their stillborn child. Equally troubling to me was the father who eulogized his adult son after he had hung himself. Words cannot express the despair of the mother whose adult son shot himself in the head. Even in those cases where people have lived an extremely long life, people don't want to say goodbye to their loved ones. Death is a marauding force that we are utterly powerless against. It is always going to be here, and there is nothing we can do about it. But according to Song of Solomon, there is something that should be stronger than death—the love that you have for your spouse. The wife in Song of Solomon says, "for love is as strong as death. . ." She is essentially saying, "My love for you is stronger than the most uncontrollable force that humanity has ever known." Their love is more powerful than even the grave. Phenomenal intimacy will follow this kind of powerful love.

Powerful love will also keep your marriage strong through the most difficult times in marriage.

"OBEDIENCE THROUGH REFINING FIRE"

"Cancer is a word I never thought I would ever hear spoken to me, but on April 15, 2014, I was diagnosed with stage III pancreatic cancer. A diagnosis of pancreatic cancer is devastating, and the struggles of this disease are debilitating. The statistics weren't positive, and I found myself starting to fear the possibility that I would not survive. Pancreatic cancer is usually terminal, with a five-year survival rate of only 7 percent. For a person of faith, however, there is nothing that God's love cannot conquer. When we walk by faith, cancer is no longer a deadly disease because of our living hope in Christ Jesus. I knew my life was in His hands, and my faith in Him would be tested beyond my limits . . . but not His. I needed to trust God and know that His perfect plan was for my benefit and His glory.

"My tumor wasn't operable, so my treatment plan was chemotherapy for six months, radiation and chemotherapy for six weeks, and then surgery. Right before each phase of my treatment, I could hear Jesus asking me, 'Do you love me?' My response was, 'Yes, Lord, I love you.' Ultimately, my body was completely broken and weakened by these treatments to the point that I was unable to care for myself. My quality of life was declining, and we weren't sure if I would live or die. Cancer is not pretty.

"My respect and admiration grow daily for my husband. Just as God has called him to love the church, he has loved me. Through this refining fire, my husband has demonstrated remarkable obedience. For two years I couldn't leave my home. I wasn't able to attend church, Bible study, or volunteer with the children. My life as I knew it was gone. For about a year, I could not even leave my bathroom. On three different occasions, I thought I was going to die. During this time, my husband has taken care of my medication and has carried me to every doctor's appointment. He has always been a step ahead of the process that I was experiencing, even the side effects of my medication. My husband served as my memory when my condition made it hard to remember. There was a point when I was so weak, all I could do was lay my hand on the Bible—then he would read God's Word to me. Praise God I have a husband who would read the Bible to me.

"Just like Jesus, he has walked this journey with me, never leaving my side. In so many ways, we are living again for the first time in years filled with compassion and love for each other. We found beauty in the ashes and blessings in our tears. God has taught us to live for today and be grateful, because tomorrow is another gift from Him and not guaranteed. As we mirror Christ's love for us, our love for each other has grown, allowing our marriage to be a testimony for Christ."

—Married 33 Years

Their Love Is as Unrelenting as the Grave

Have you ever noticed that nobody ever comes out of the grave? Once people go in the grave, they stay in the grave until the resurrection. The grave always holds the dead; this is what makes the resurrection of Jesus from the grave so absolutely amazing. In Song of Solomon, she leverages this well-known reality to illustrate the predictable strength of her love for her husband. She says, "its jealousy unyielding as the grave. . ." (8:6). Her point is simply this: "Just as the grave never releases the dead, I will never release you." She is describing the kind of love that is not contingent upon him being the perfect husband or the most successful man in town. Her love is so strong that it does not matter that he is an imperfect sinner who will make many mistakes as a husband. Her love is not based upon his good looks or her happiness. Her love is an uncontrollable force that will not let him go! Marriages would not dissolve quite so easily today if more people loved their spouses in this manner. But in the strange event that you are neither impressed with this love nor inspired to emulate it for your spouse, let's move on to the next metaphor, which I think you will like even more.

Their Love Is like Fire

The wife in Song of Solomon also compares her love to fire, "It burns like a blazing fire, like a mighty flame. Many waters cannot quench love; rivers cannot sweep it away" (8:6–7). When was the last time you saw a raging fire? Fires can burn with such intensity that they are nearly impossible to extinguish. Fires can effortlessly engulf houses, buildings, and entire ecosystems. Despite all of the technology that exists today, a raging forest fire can leave well-equipped firefighters desperately praying for rain. What a powerful image to explain her love for her husband! Her love rages with white-hot intensity for her husband. But given the right environmental factors, every fire can eventually be extinguished. To this reasonable line of thinking, she says, "Not so fast." So persuaded in the strength of her love that she says "mighty waters" and "rivers" cannot extinguish it away. Did you know that at Niagara Falls, over 600,000 gallons of water fall over the edge every second? She says not even torrential water like that of Niagara Falls could tamp out my love for my husband. Some fires just keep burning!

There is an underground coal seam fire in Centralia, Pennsylvania, that has been burning for over fifty-three years. Many believe the fire started when people in the town burned what remained of an old landfill in 1962. Though they were able to extinguish the fire on the ground level, a literal inferno blazed underneath the ground. Apparently, this landfill also once served as a strip mine and was attached to an underground maze of mining tunnels full of coal. With no way to extinguish the underground inferno, the citizens of Centralia were forced to move. By some accounts, there is enough coal underground to keep the fire going for another 250 years.[2] Your love for your spouse needs to burn like the inferno in Centralia!

Maybe this is a good opportunity to stop and ask the simple ques-

---

2. James Cave, "This Abandoned Pennsylvania Town Has Been on Fire for 53 Years," January 9, 2017, http://www.huffingtonpost.com/entry/this-abandoned-pennsylvania-town-has-been-on-fire-for-53-years_us_55df6490e4b08dc09486d4a0.

tion, "How is the love in your marriage?" Does it sizzle with white-hot intensity or is it fizzling out? Why is it that some fires are so hard to stop and others are nearly impossible to start? I love grilling steaks out back, and I've learned a few things in the process! You cannot just light a match, throw it on the charcoal, and expect to have steaks in a few minutes. Sometimes you have to nurture the fire. That fire needs oxygen, and you have to fan the flame. I wonder if your love for your spouse needs to be fanned.

What are you doing to fan the flame of your love for your spouse? Are you spending enough time with your spouse alone? Maybe it's time to call a babysitter or arrange to enjoy a long weekend in a cabin somewhere. One of the greatest things you can do to fan the love in your marriage is to serve each other in sacrificial ways. This will mean something very different in every marriage. Try watching the children so that you can give your spouse an opportunity to do something they enjoy. Maybe you can take over cooking or cleaning for a few days. Maybe you could volunteer to help with the laundry. These sacrificial acts of service will go a long way in giving your spouse the emotional space they need in order to pay more attention to the marriage. But by far the greatest thing that you can do to fan the flame of your love for your spouse is to walk with the Lord Jesus on a daily basis. It is God who transforms you into the spouse that God wants you to be. Over time, God will transform the way you respond to your spouse when you are tired, frustrated, or exasperated. As God transforms you, you will become increasingly irresistible to your spouse. It is only through walking with Jesus that we cultivate the ability to love like this couple in Song of Solomon.

Sometimes, when you light a fire, you need to rearrange the fire in order for it to burn well. You may need to add some more kindling, take a log off, or reposition the wood. If your marriage is experiencing great difficulties, perhaps it's time to consider making some significant changes. Maybe it's time to get rid of some habits that are proving detrimental to the health of your marriage. Is it time to rearrange your priorities? Do you need to change how you spend your money?

One of the best ways to make sure a fire burns hot is to put something *really* hot right next to it. Heat loves heat and fire loves fire. There are so many happening marriages in the church. Maybe it's time to plant your marriage in a church where you spend time with those who can teach you the things they have learned about marriage. Join a Sunday school class. Start attending a small group with those whose marriages are burning brightly. Learn from others what it takes to have a flourishing marriage. Ask them, "What makes your marriage tick?" Tell them, "We want our marriage to flourish like yours. Teach us what we need to learn." I think marriage is always going to be challenging, but it does not have to be as challenging as we sometimes make it. Plant your life in church, feast on God's Word, and fellowship with others who have great marriages.

Their Love Is Worth More than Gold and Silver

Do you and your spouse argue regularly about money? If you do, you are not alone. Every couple must work through how to manage their family's finances according to Scripture. Husbands and wives need to learn to communicate when it comes to spending and budgeting. They need to be on the same page when it comes to the standard of living they will enjoy. Unfortunately, for some couples, the subject of finances is not something they have to work through; it's something that they are willing to leave for. In a world that idolizes money, we shouldn't be surprised that many people would walk away from their spouses for financial reasons. Some women have essentially said, "If you cannot provide me the standard of living that I want, somebody else can." The apostle Paul was right when he said that the "love of money is a root of all kinds of evil. Some people, eager for money, have wandered from the faith and pierced themselves with many griefs" (1 Tim. 6:10). The example of the couple in Song of Solomon is refreshing on this score.

Listen to what she says about her husband in Song of Solomon chapter 8: "If one were to give all the wealth of one's house for love, it would be utterly scorned" (8:7). It seems like in today's world money can buy anything. Just because something is not for sale does not mean that it cannot be bought for the right price. I, for example, don't have a For Sale sign in front of my house, but I promise you that if somebody offered me three times what it was worth, I would sell it in an instant. I think there are many people who would walk away from their spouse given the right financial motivation. But this woman's love for her husband is so strong that all the money in the world could not buy it. Not only would she not accept it, she would scorn the money! Let's talk about the Hebrew word translated "scorn" for a moment. Proverbs 30:17 says, "The eye that mocks a father, that scorns an aged mother, will be pecked out by the ravens of the valley, will be eaten by the vultures." Do you see how serious it can be to scorn? According to this verse, scorning one's parent was so egregious that it was deserving of death with the added punishment of their eyes pecked out by the vultures. This is exactly how forcefully she would reject any financial motivation to leave her husband.

Loving in this manner is a self-crucifying experience. Your flesh will reject the kind of self-sacrificing work it will take to love like this. Your mind will try to talk you out of dying to yourself in the ways that it will take to love like this. How on earth could we ever love like this?

"MARRIAGE IN THE LIGHT OF ETERNITY"

"God sustained me with His Word in the time of struggle for my marriage. 'The house of the righteous will stand' (Prov. 12:7) became my song. 'Praise be to the Lord, for he showed me the wonders of his love when I was in a city under siege' was my position (Ps. 31:21). However, the turning point in my heart happened one morning as I sat on my front porch. Our daughter had asked me to search for names in our family history for our first granddaughter.

"My husband's family has kept their history since 1845, and the two volumes include 1,552 pages. In the quiet early morning, I began to see my marriage in the light of eternity. As I looked over the pages of the book, I saw so many broken families. The repeated word—divorce—

seemed to be shouting to me as those broken families over 170 years marched in front of my eyes.

"In that moment, God forever changed my focus about marriage. What is my marriage about? In my heart I knew I never wanted my grandchildren to read those words next to our names. The realization was that my marriage was not about my happiness or fulfillment. Marriage is all about the preciousness of our covenant before God. The words spoken forty years earlier in commitment were suddenly fresh just like the day.

"Many difficult situations were affecting our marriage. My husband traveled for his job, and he was angry about the difficulty that it created, but neither of us was effective at resolving conflict or communicating. We had not seen examples of good marriages with our parents. We both knew that we did not want to raise our children in a strife-filled home. We did not want our children to feel knots in their stomachs because of anger spoken or unspoken. Consequently, we had not learned to resolve conflict effectively. Our daughter has remarked that the only time she saw us angry was on the way to church because Mom could not wait to get there and Dad was driving slow. For that, we're so thankful!

"It was a great relief to know that my marriage was not just about happiness. My commitment was to God and to the covenant of marriage. Nothing changed for us, but my marriage was, from that point, in God's hands. God began to transform our relationship in tiny incremental steps. It was a healing time for our marriage. Today we have been blessed with eleven grandchildren . . . and my husband is the best grandfather on the planet."

—Married 48 Years

God's Love for You in Christ

I suppose it does seem rather impossible to love like this. I don't know about you, but I can be so selfish and petty. I hate how irritable and impatient I can be with my wife. We are all so weak, and life can be incredibly difficult. There never seems to be enough time in a day, so we often feel pulled in many directions. It's not that you don't want to love your spouse in the right ways, it just seems difficult. With bills to pay and mouths to feed, it can be hard to invest a lot of time and energy into your spouse. With life being as challenging and unpredictable as it is, is it even impossible to have a love stronger than death? The simple answer is "no" in your own strength. We cannot love like this in our own strength! But, with God's help, we can love like this, because this is exactly the kind of love that we have received from God.

God's love for you is strong; so strong that he slayed His Son on the cross for you. God has "lavished" love on you despite that fact that you are a sinner who deserves death and hell (1 John 3:1). The Bible teaches that all have sinned and fallen short of the glory of God (Rom. 3:23) and that the wages of this sin is death (Rom. 6:23). God's love for you burns like a fire. All of the flames of hell could not extinguish God's love for you. God's love for you is stronger than death; it is more unyielding than the grave. And the wonderful thing is, once you respond to God's love by putting your faith in Jesus Christ, nothing could ever separate you from Him.

> Who shall separate us from the love of Christ? Shall trouble or hardship or persecution or famine or nakedness or danger or sword? No, in all these things we are more than conquerors through him who loved us. For I am convinced that neither death nor life, neither angels nor demons, neither the present nor the future, nor any powers, neither height nor depth, nor anything else in all creation, will be able to separate us from the love of God that is in Christ Jesus our Lord. (Rom. 8:35, 37–39)

If you have never trusted Jesus Christ for the forgiveness of your sins, I want to invite you to ask God, even now, for Him to save you. The Bible says that "everyone who calls on the name of the Lord will be saved" (Rom. 10:13). Nothing in the world could improve your marriage like becoming one of God's children through your unwavering faith in Jesus Christ. Every problem in your marriage is secondary to the far more important need to be reconciled to God.

If you have already received this love by faith in what Jesus did for you on the cross, you can give it as you trust in the power of the Holy Spirit who raised Jesus from the dead. Only God, through the power of the Holy Spirit, can help you love your spouse like this! It's only by receiving this love that husbands can love their wives as Christ loved the church, dying daily for their spouse (Eph. 5:25). Walk daily with Jesus Christ through His Word and ask God for His strength to love your wife like this.

Sexual intimacy can never flourish outside a strong abiding love. If your sexual intimacy is not what you want it to be, cultivate a stronger love for your spouse. Walk with Christ and ask Him to teach you how to love your spouse more sacrificially. Ask Him to give you the desire to love your spouse in the ways that they need to be loved. Ask the Lord to open your eyes to the uniqueness of your spouse and to the ways that you can demonstrate your love for them. Pray for God to strengthen the bond that holds you together.

Wounded Love

Those you love the most have the potential to hurt you the most. Your love for them intensifies the pain. Love and pain in marriage sometimes stand side by side with proportional strength. If you allow this pain to fester into unresolved bitterness, you will destroy any hope of achieving the kind of intimacy presented in Song of Solomon.

Are you hanging on to any bitterness in your marriage that you need to confess? Are you withholding forgiveness from your spouse? Forgiveness is not optional for couples longing for the caliber of intimacy described in Song of Solomon. It's amazing how even the smallest bitter root can greatly diminish your desire for your spouse. It can be something as small as your spouse never acknowledging how hard you worked to clean the house. Or how you felt disrespected when they rudely corrected you in front of everybody. It sounds so petty, yet these are the kinds of things that can sabotage sexual intimacy. In other cases, the issues are not insignificant. Maybe you've struggled to forgive your spouse for what they did sexually with somebody else before you were married. Or maybe you've struggled to come to terms with something they said to you in your latest heated argument. With those stinging words still ringing in your head, incredible intimacy will be handicapped. An unforgiving heart will be an insurmountable obstacle. Do you have unforgiveness in your heart toward your spouse? What are you holding on to? What keeps you from wanting to be intimate with your spouse?

When it comes to forgiving, it's not just about removing the obstacles to intimacy. Forgiving your spouse is the obligation of every true believer in Jesus Christ. The fact that you're married to the person who has wounded you does not give you a pass. Admittedly, it may mean that they've hurt you more grievously. But this does not give you a warrant to persist in bitterness. Far from abdicating you of the responsibility to forgive, the fact that you are married to the person who hurt you makes forgiveness that much more important. In the Sermon on the Mount, Jesus taught that we can expect forgiveness from God as we forgive others (Matt. 6:14). The apostle Paul also connected the issue of forgiving others with receiving God's forgiveness saying, "Be kind and compassionate to one another, forgiving each other, just as in Christ God forgave you" (Eph. 4:32).

I'm sure we can all agree that forgiveness is right, but that does not mean that it's easy. It's difficult to address the issue of forgiveness in marriage, not knowing the circumstances that surround your situation. One thing is clear: not every situation is identical. There may be aspects of your situation that fall far outside the bounds of what this section addresses. If your spouse has done something truly egregious that falls outside of the normal struggles that couples experience, you may need to take additional steps not included below. But when it comes to everyday frustrations and challenges in your marriage relationship, the best place to start is always with prayer.

Pray about it. When it comes to forgiveness, there is no substitute for spending a lot of time in prayer. Like any other act of obedience, you need God's help. Chances are, you will ruminate endlessly over what they did or didn't do without God's help. Every attempt at working through your anger may only stoke the flames of unforgiveness in your heart. Satan will likely work overtime to remind you of all the reasons why your spouse does not deserve your forgiveness. You don't have the capacity to forgive without God's help. Ask God to give you the strength to forgive your spouse. Your heavenly Father is a master when it comes to forgiveness. You can't change your heart, only God can. As you spend time with God, He will change your heart, your mind, and your attitude toward your spouse. Absent time with the Lord, you will likely continue to struggle with unforgiveness. I want to share a simple prayer that you can use when you are struggling to forgive: "Father, I choose to forgive, but help me to forgive."

Talk about it. Learning to forgive can be a process. Along the way in this journey, you may need to be honest about what's troubling you. I'm not encouraging you to air every petty, selfish grievance with your spouse. In fact, when the grace of Jesus reigns in a marriage, you don't have to dredge up and hammer out every trivial problem. Not every issue warrants a big discussion. But there are some challenges in marriage that cannot be resolved without talking. It's not fair to your spouse to leave them in the dark about something that's creating division in your marriage. If you clam up, whatever they imagine is wrong with you might be way worse than the real issue. You definitely don't want your spouse wondering if you even still love them. You may need to say something along the lines of "I am having a tough time getting over what you did. I'm not saying this to make you feel guilty, but I need you to know what's going on in my heart." It's not about dredging up the past for the sake of shaming your spouse. Instead, it's about honesty. Even this might spark a helpful discussion that can bring this issue to a smooth resolution.

Forgive again. What most people don't understand about forgiveness is that it is not always a onetime act of obedience. What did Jesus say about forgiveness? Jesus taught us to forgive "seventy times seven" (Matt. 18:22). Or, in other words, you need to forgive over and over and over. Jesus also taught us that God will not forgive us of our sins if we do not forgive one another their sins (Matt. 6:5). There may be days that you have to forgive every hour on the hour. This does not mean that you failed to forgive the first time. It just means that you are deeply wounded by a person that you live with, a person you see every day of your life.

Get counseling. I have always thought it was strange that couples receive counseling before they wed but ignore this logical step when they need it most: after they wed. I've noticed in premarital counseling that couples don't always know what to ask me. It's after you have lived with somebody that you realize how little you actually knew about the other person and about what marriage required. When a marriage is rocked by problems, oftentimes people wait too long to get help. Then, having waited too long, people will come and see me when there is little that can be done to salvage their marriage.

There is no shame in seeing a counselor. You don't feel bad about seeing the doctor when you're sick. So don't attach any shame to seeing a counselor when your marriage is ill. Your marriage is of inestimable value. It is worth fighting for. Don't suffer in silence. Call your pastor and sit down with him first. This is always a good place to start. If your situation requires ongoing counseling, or if it falls outside of his level of expertise, he may refer you to a Christian counselor who can help guide you through the process of forgiveness.

Forgive until it hurts. When it comes to forgiveness, if it doesn't hurt, you're not doing it right. A wise man once told me that true forgiveness will feel like twisting a knife that's already been plunged into your stomach. If it hurts bad enough, you know that you are doing it right. Consider what forgiveness cost our heavenly Father. It cost Him His Son. It will cost you greatly to forgive your spouse. But the benefits will be freedom, joy, and unity in your marriage. If you choose to harbor bitterness, you will also find pain. But it will be the kind of pain that breeds contempt.

Acknowledge your own sin. So often when we get caught up in thinking about somebody else's sin, we forget our own. This is what Jesus meant when He talked about removing the log out of your own eye before you address the speck in your brother's eye (Matt. 7:3–5). I have found it so much easier to forgive when I realize how much I have been forgiven. My desire to withhold forgiveness is sometimes rooted in a false sense of self-righteousness. If you find yourself saying things such as "I would have never done that," or, "I could have never been so hurtful," it may mean that you are also struggling to see your own sin. Is your pride and selfishness any better than your spouse's sin? Have you not been guilty of the very same thing? Have you treated other people in the same way your spouse treated you? Even if you have not been guilty of the same kind of sin, wouldn't that be evidence of God's grace and not your goodness? We can be so quick to receive grace but so slow to give it.

Thank God. Thanking God for your spouse is one of the best ways to change your heart toward them. Instead of sitting around thinking about how they have disappointed you, start making a list of all of the ways they exceed what you deserve in a spouse. Give thanks to God for the character qualities that you have come to love and admire. Most likely, you have many things to be thankful for in your spouse. A grateful heart will quell so many of your negative thoughts.

Move on. I think it's important to work through problems in your marriage. I encourage you to talk about it, pray about it, and go to counseling. But, at some point, you need to move on. The Bible teaches that without wood a fire goes out (Prov. 26:20). Do you want your spouse to throw your mistakes back in your face? If you make a habit of bringing up their sin, it will create a toxic dynamic in your marriage where nothing can flourish. Resist the urge to bring every argument and discussion back to the thing that you have already forgiven them for.

Remember, your spouse is probably already struggling with feeling forgiven. It's your job to help them walk in forgiveness. How can they experience God's grace if you refuse to give it to them? But some will say, "My spouse does not deserve it." Isn't that the point of grace? Grace is favor that is unmerited. Giving your spouse grace is one of the most gospel-centric things you can do.

Today, start working toward forgiveness. The longer you wait, the more difficult it will become. Don't assume that things will get better on their own. Don't ignore the problem. You do not want to miss out on the blessings of forgiving your spouse. What a shame to live in an unhappy marriage when you could experience the joys of giving grace. The benefits of working through your problems will far outweigh whatever it cost you to forgive. The glorious intimacy described in Song of Solomon is not attainable for those who persist in unforgiveness. Regardless of how you have been wounded, you have the opportunity to love. As Gary Chapman notes, "Love doesn't erase the past, but makes the future different."[3]

"WHO IS THIS MAN?"

He left me! Who is this man? I thought I knew him . . .

"Arriving from Texas in the Rocky Mountains required a careful choice of activities in dealing with sudden altitude changes and much lower temperatures. My husband and I said yes to an invitation from a seasoned local to snowshoe in the mountains. Our trek began in the mountains at 10,000 feet above sea level.

"I quickly realized that I could not keep pace with the other three trekkers. Our hiking companion Ronald realized that I had no stamina, along with some difficulty breathing. He noticed that I was struggling to make it through the snow to the woods above. He kindly stayed behind to look after me while my husband was swishing through the snow, fully engaged in conversation with the local outdoorswoman—a blonde, trim, divorced, and knowledgeable woman who was ever so attentive to him. Realizing I needed help, I cupped my hands around my mouth and shouted, 'PLEASE, A REST!' There was too much distance for them to hear my plea. Why wasn't my husband checking on me? So intent on the local's insight, he never turned his head to see how far behind we were. In my mind, he had committed adultery.

---

3. Gary Chapman, *The Five Love Languages: How to Express Heartfelt Commitment to Your Mate* (Chicago: Northfield Publishing, 2004), 143.

"After a long hard climb, Ronald and I arrived at the top of the climb where the two trailblazers were waiting. When asked to return to the car, 'the long way or short?' my husband eagerly spoke up that he wanted to go back the long way. 'Ugh,' I thought.

"After returning to the car, the trip back to the condo was colder than any Arctic spot—my husband abandoned me. I got my book, shut the bedroom door, and lived alone.

"The ten days following our trip home were nothing but hell on earth. Neither of us were able to sleep or eat. There was no peace. We slept apart, and my husband would have to close the door to his bedroom to keep from hearing me cry. He feared strongly that forty-five years of marriage had been destroyed in just two hours. He realized that only God's intervention and grace could restore this marriage.

"So he committed to ten hours of fasting and prayer. He prayed, read Scripture, and documented all God showed him that day. He realized that he had sinned against his wife, allowing the sin of ego to override the love he felt for his wife. The next day, Sunday, we went to church, where our pastor preached on wisdom from Ecclesiastes 9:13–18. From the text, he concluded (1) wisdom is better than strength, (2) we want power and position, (3) if you want power in your marriage, seek wisdom, and (4) the Enemy is trying to build siege works against your marriage. My husband knew that this sermon was meant for him. After the sermon, he went to the altar to pray, and I FOLLOWED! It was the first positive thing to happen in ten days.

"On the way home from church, he confessed that he had wanted to prove that at age sixty-five, he could *still do it* at the cost of possibly destroying our marriage. Through the sermon, God had confirmed for him everything God had taught him the day before. I immediately responded, and communication began to open up for the first time.

"One late afternoon, I laid my body in his lap and told him that I was choosing to lay all of my hurt and grief on the altar. God taught me that I do not deserve God's forgiveness just as my husband did not deserve my forgiveness. I could not forgive him on my own, but God helped me, a process that is ongoing. God's wisdom, not logic or emotion, saved our marriage—TO GOD BE THE GLORY."

—Married 45 Years

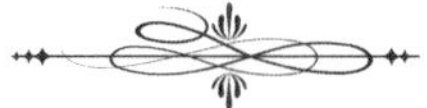

Strong Love, Strong Churches

Jesus taught that the world would know who His disciples were by their love for one another (John 13:35). The world won't know we are Christians by our magnificent buildings or our soaring budgets. It also won't know it necessarily by our accomplished and polished preachers or by the number of programs that the church offers the community. The world will know you and me by the love that we show one another. Believers in Jesus Christ need a strong, unquenchable love for one another. If we can't show Christian love in our marriages, how can we ever hope to show it to our brothers and sisters in Christ? Emphasizing sexual intimacy in your marriage will go a long way toward prioritizing the love that you have for your spouse. As your love for your spouse grows through mutual sacrifice and service, you will have a greater capacity to love others in your Christian community. It's this love that will shine brightly in a very dark and desperate world. If people cannot find love in Christian marriages or in the body of Christ, where will they find it?

Homework

1. Name some difficult circumstances that have demonstrated the strength of your love for each other.
2. Ask each other the following question: "What are some practical ways that I demonstrate my strong love for you?"
3. Complete the following sentence: "I feel your strong love for me when you . . ."
4. Complete the following sentence: "My desire to make love increases when you . . ."
5. Discuss what would make you both feel more secure in your marriage.

A Prayer for You

"Father, we thank you for your strong love for us. Thank you for sending your Son to die on the cross for us. We rejoice that your love is stronger than death and more unyielding than the grave! We delight in the knowledge that your love is like a consuming fire that blazes with white-hot intensity for us. With your fiery love, you have saved us from the flames of hell.

"Thank you for giving us your Holy Spirit to help us love each other. We pray that the intensity of our love for each other would show the world your love. Teach us to love each other. Stir within our hearts a desire to love with greater strength. Forgive us for all the ways in which our love for each other has been weak. Forgive us for the selfishness that we have allowed to creep in and taint our devotion to each other. Help us to be sacrificial in our love toward each other. By your Holy Spirit, give us the strength to resist our flesh. Help us to understand our spouse and the ways that they long to be loved.

"Help our love for each other to be patient and kind, never envious or boastful. Help us not to be quickly provoked toward anger or to keep record of wrongs. Empower us to bear all things, believe all things, hope all things and endure all things. May our love for each other never fail (1 Cor. 13:4–7).

"Within the confines of our growing love for each other, cause our sexual relationship to flourish in wonderful ways. May our love for each other prompt us to show in physical ways our love for each other. May the strength of our loving bond destroy all of the unhealthy inhibitions that keep us from experiencing the best of sexual intimacy. We pray that our sexual relationship would fuel our growing love for each other. In Jesus' name, Amen."

Chapter 6

SEX IS THE FRUIT OF A STRONG FRIENDSHIP

Scripture Reading: Song of Solomon 6

I bet you've heard those dreaded words, "Let's just be friends," like nearly everybody else at some point along the way. These words send every budding relationship to a screeching halt. No matter how gently these words are communicated, they always have the same result. "Let's just be friends" often means that person wants want nothing to do with you. Friendships are rarely strengthened after those dreaded words are uttered. But friendship in marriage is another matter altogether.

In marriage, friendship is a prelude to the closest kind of intimacy. Friendship is the highway that leads into the most amazing sex life. There is no such thing as "just friends" in marriage because friendship leads to wonderful intimacy. In marriage, "let's be friends" is the opportunity of a lifetime. These two in Song of Solomon are not just lovers, they are friends!

The daughters of Jerusalem appear to challenge her affection for her husband, saying twice, "How is your beloved better than others?" (5:9). This is probably the biggest "softball question" she could have received. She is loaded with answers for anyone who will listen. After waxing eloquent about how respectable, strong, and handsome he is, she ends with this phrase: "This is my friend." At this, the daughters of Jerusalem do not say another word. This description meant far more to her than his wavy hair and his sculpted body. She had what every other woman of Jerusalem wanted: a best friend.

Let's explore their friendship.

They Love Hearing Each Other's Voice

I have a feeling that if this couple lived in the twenty-first century, they would be texting and calling each other constantly. While apart, they would be video chatting up a storm. Can you imagine the number of flirtatious emojis they would be hurling back and forth at each other on their smartphones? Do you love the sound of your lover's voice? In Song of Solomon, his wife has so much to say, yet he never tires of hearing her voice. He says, "Let me hear your voice" (2:14; 8:13).

Judging from how rudely some married couples talk with each other, it's clear that they don't always like the sound of their lover's voice. Les and Leslie Parrott describe an unfortunate transformation that takes place in many marriages: "When we first married, we were the epitome of kindness and sensitivity. But somewhere along the line, without any effort on our part, a side of us revealed that we had become surprisingly testy, touchy, and downright irritable."[1] I think most married people can relate to this. What about you? Do you tend to roll your eyes when your spouse says something that you disapprove of? Do you find yourself rudely correcting your spouse over minutia when he tells a story in public? Do you ignore your wife's calls while you are at work? Are you quick to fire off sarcastic remarks that disparage each other? Are you quick to argue every time your wife disagrees with you? Do you register your irritation with loud sighs throughout the day in conversation with him? Do you leave the room when she starts talking?

It's possible to become so accustomed to being rude to your spouse

---

1. Les and Leslie Parrott, *I Love You More* (Grand Rapids: Zondervan, 2005), 98.

that you don't even know that you do it. Those who interact rudely with each other during the day do not go home and have sensational sex at night. Rudeness in a relationship is a barometer to everybody else that reads, "We have a terribly unsatisfying sex life."

It's time to get back to the days when the very hint of your lover's voice made your belly do somersaults. If you are anything like Stephanie and me, you stayed on the phone for hours just to hear each other's voice when you first started dating. Even after all these years of marriage, I still want to hear her voice when I'm on the road. I want to tell her all about my day and hear all about hers. The day just doesn't feel complete without hearing her speak. I want to hear her voice because it gives me a window into her heart. Just by listening to her voice, I know how her day is going. I can hear joy, disappointment, and excitement if I pay close attention. I can tell if the kids have been difficult to manage and whether or not she was able to make time for her art project. I love to hear her voice.

Strive to stay in love with your lover's voice. Talk to your spouse. Be open and honest about what's going on in your life. Give your spouse the opportunity to know how you are changing and growing and learning. Mutual curiosity is one of the things that "made dating so intoxicating" before marriage.[2] Tell your spouse what the Lord has been teaching and how He's been encouraging you. Don't just audibly listen to your spouse, but do your best to understand what their heart is saying. Be sure to listen to each other in the morning before you go your separate ways. It's also important to end the day well. Make your spouse a priority when they come home from work. Stop what you are doing and give them the attention they need. Always make sure that your spouse feels heard. Failing to listen to your spouse can "sabotage intimacy."[3] Listening is one of the loudest ways to demonstrate

---

2. Gary Thomas, *Cherish: The One Word That Changes Everything for Your Marriage* (Grand Rapids: Zondervan, 2017), 119.
3. Gary Chapman, *The 4 Seasons of Marriage: Secrets to a Lasting Marriage* (Wheaton, IL: Tyndale House, 2012), 108.

your love. Do these things every day so your friendship can grow and flourish.

You know that you are best friends when you want to tell your spouse everything. I tell Stephanie nearly everything about my day. Not talking to her about things in my life is an unsettling feeling for me. Talking to my wife helps me face the challenges of life. When it comes to good news, I can't fully experience the joy until I share it with her. Why? Because she is my best friend. She always wants to hear what I have to say. She wants to hear about my day and how everything went. In the evenings, Stephanie and I love to take walks up and down our driveway. We dream talk and try to find solutions to parenting issues. Sometimes we will brew some hot tea and enjoy a cup on the back porch before bed. We treasure these moments.

You know that you are best friends when you are able to speak the truth. Friends speak the truth because friendship demands it. I know I can trust my wife to say even the things that I don't want to hear. She would never say anything to intentionally harm me, nor would I to her. But any healthy friendship requires an unfettered gracious truthfulness. In fact, there is no way for your friendship to grow if you don't speak the truth to each other. Does your spouse experience the freedom to speak truth to you? How do you respond when your spouse tells you something that you need to hear? The Bible says that an honest answer is like a kiss on the lips (Prov. 24:26). If your wife tells you that you are being selfish, there is a pretty good chance that you're being selfish. If your husband tells you that you are acting prideful, there's a good chance that you're being prideful. There ought to be enough love in a relationship where you can say these things without an explosive reaction. Marriage should be safe enough to say the things that need to be said.

You know you are best friends when you share openly about your dreams. Friends always champion each other's dreams. In the ministry, I have encouraged and prayed for my brothers who were pursuing their dreams. I am always in their corner, encouraging them to succeed. If my wife is my friend, then surely I would treat her in the same way. She has laid down so much so that I could finish my education, manage a growing ministry, and write books. I want to be the kind of husband who encourages my wife to chase after her dreams. I want Stephanie to be able to draw, paint, and finish that children's book she began. I want her to have a great art studio to work in so she can complete her project. If your spouse is your friend, you will help her achieve her dreams. Friendship also requires spending a lot of time together.

They Love Spending Time Together

When you are best friends, you love spending time together. Time together is not a chore or a tedious requirement of marriage. Spending time with each other is one of the best things about marriage. These lovers in Song of Solomon *love* being together. In chapter 1, she asks him, "Tell me, you whom I love, where you graze your flock and where you rest your sheep at midday" (1:7). She wants to know where he's grazing the flocks so she can go and have lunch with him. She also wants to go to the vineyard so she can experience the beauty of the changing season with her best friend. The budding of the flowers in the vineyard just did not have the same beauty without her best friend by her side.

Their desire to spend time with each other is also evident in the fact that they are constantly wanting to get away. From the very beginning of the book, the wife says, "Take me with you, let us hurry . . ." (1:4). In fact, Song of Solomon ends this way as well, with her beckoning him, "Come away, my beloved, and be like a gazelle or like a young stag on the spice-laden mountains" (8:14). He shares his longing to be with his bride and calls out to her repeatedly, saying variations of "Come away my beautiful one" (2:10, 13; 4:8). We will talk later about the sexual implications of these invitations, but for now consider what this says about their friendship. Their relationship demanded time alone with each other. No friendship can flourish if it does not have time to develop. Your relationship with your spouse demands the same.

You know you are best friends when you can't wait to get home from work. I love my job, but every day I look forward to getting home to see my wife. For me, being with Stephanie is the essence of what it means to be home. I enjoy traveling to preach God's Word, but every time I leave, I cannot wait to get home. I don't want to hang out with the guys every Friday night or spend an entire day away from my wife at some ball game. I don't have any interest in leaving my wife every weekend to go fishing or to freeze to death in a deer blind. I want to be with my wife.

You know you are best friends when you love doing things together. When I'm with Stephanie, it doesn't matter how boring a task is, we just enjoy each other's company. We joke sometimes about how we love to be boring together. We love taking drives and looking at homes, taking walks, and having nice quiet evenings at home. The crazy thing is, it's not boring at all to us. We love being together. I would rather spend time with Stephanie than any other person on the planet. Marriage is all about the joy of being together with your best friend.

"MY LIFELONG BEST FRIEND"

A simple prayer that was prayed by a very confused young woman of eighteen years: "Please, dear God, send someone to just love me."

"I grew up in a home filled with child abuse. As a result of my testimony in court, my father was sent to prison. Five of us children had been raised by a cruel and heartless father, a man determined to make us fearfully obedient —and he had succeeded.

"I am sharing this because I want you to know that the Lord heard that simple prayer fifty-one years ago, and He brought my dear husband into my life. God knew it would take a special person to love me and care for me because of my basic temperament and the baggage I brought into the marriage. I first met my husband on a blind date, and we both felt a special tenderness and love that were based on respect and admiration. We have never liked to be away from each other. We have a wonderful friendship now of fifty-one years that continues to grow as we face even more challenges through the aging process.

"Through the years I have told so many people that the glue that holds our marriage together is the Holy Spirit. We both surrendered our lives to the Lord Jesus Christ early in our marriage. The One who put us together has been faithful to strengthen our love for each other. He has kept us together through the difficult times in our marriage, the most recent being the homegoing of our granddaughter. My husband cries easily, but not me. I was beaten repeatedly for crying . . . some of that baggage again. In a strange way, the tragedy of our granddaughter's death has brought us even closer as we continue to share our tears and deepest feelings. When I prayed that simple prayer for someone to love me, God heard my prayer and sent me my lifelong best friend!"

—Married 51 Years

Their Friendship Is Refreshing

You are a Spring... a sealed Fountain (4:12).

There is a huge difference between a smelly cattle tank filled with animal filth and a spring-fed creek that nourishes plants and wildlife for miles. What do you want to be to your spouse? You have a choice to make in your marriage. These lovers refresh each other in Song of Solomon.

The very thought of her does not exhaust or drain him. He is refreshed by his wife. He's not tinkering endlessly in the garage or intentionally working late to avoid his wife. She is a garden "spring" to him. This Hebrew word translated "fountain" conveys a powerful image of blessing. This is the very same word used to describe the fountains of the deep that God opened up when He flooded the earth (Gen. 7:11; 8:2). In other words, it's not the kind of word that you might use to describe a natural spring that only trickles. It's also a word used to convey the rich blessings that we have through the Lord. It was God who satisfied the thirst of an entire nation by turning a rock into a "fountain" (Ps. 104:10). Isaiah refers to the "fountains of salvation" (Isa. 12:3), and Joel prophesies a day when a "fountain will flow from out of the Lord's house" (Joel 3:18).[4] When he thinks of his wife, he sees a garden full of rich blessings. If you want to cultivate a powerful friendship, seek to be a garden spring to your spouse.

Let me ask you a question. What makes you want to spend time with some friends and not others? What makes you call, text, and stay in touch with some friends while you simultaneously let other relationships go? What makes you willing to inconvenience yourself to see some friends while you are unwilling to do anything to spend time with others? Those whom you spend the most time with are very likely the same ones who refresh you the most! Strive to be that refreshing person for your spouse. The most important thing that you can start doing today is to spend time with the Lord through His Word and prayer.

Walk with Christ. Walking with Christ through His Word and prayer will have a dramatic impact on your marriage. You cannot be refreshing to your husband or your wife if you are not being refreshed in the Word of God. On your own you do not have the personal resources to remain a source of refreshment to your spouse. The natural challenges of life and marriage will deplete your resources, leaving you empty-handed. When you feel depleted you are more likely to be needy, short-tempered, irritable, and unreasonable . . . not exactly the ingredients of a refreshing marriage. God, on the other hand, has a limitless supply of everything that you need to love your spouse well. It's not possible to exhaust the Lord's resources. As the Lord fills you with love, patience, and grace to overflowing, you will be able to represent Christ to your spouse. If you want to be a conduit of blessing to your spouse, spend time with the Lord.

Don't be Critical. The opposite of refreshment is found in the book of Proverbs, where the contentious woman is compared to a

---

4. See also the usage of the term in Ps. 87:7. Foreigners who acknowledge the Lord will be included amongst God's people and will sing, "All of my fountains are in you."

leaky roof (Prov. 19:13; 27:15). Do you want to be a constant dripping or a refreshing stream? When he gets home from work, do you quickly remind him of every errand he forgot to do? Do you instantly tell him everything that is wrong with the house and with the kids? Do you nitpick him with sarcastic comments that subtly express how he irritates you? Or do you take the time to connect with him? Do you ask him about his day and encourage him? Do you make him so happy he wants to come home to you? A constant dripping will drive your husband away, but a refreshing stream will lure him in. Remember that men are not immune to a critical spirit; it's just that we don't typically refer to it as nagging.

Whereas women tend to nag, men nitpick. Men—do you find yourself criticizing your wife's cooking? Are you quick to find fault with the way that your wife cleans? Do you go out of your way to correct everything that she says? Some men have subtler ways of reminding their wife that she is not meeting their expectations. Do you insert witty, sarcastic comments into conversations to draw a laugh? Do you belittle her efforts in front of the children or, even worse, your parents? Do you take jabs at your wife on social networking? Most of the time, your wife needs encouragement, not correction. Your critical spirit will destroy your best efforts at cultivating a deep, lasting friendship.

A Lasting Relationship

Intimacy in marriage flourishes when a husband and wife enjoy a strong, lasting friendship. Your buddies from work and acquaintances from around town will come and go, but your spouse will always be there. Even your best buddies through school will eventually fade from your radar. You probably won't always fish with the same guys or shop with the same group of girls in ten years. Even with some of your relatives, your friendships might experience major changes. Friends at work will come and go. Regardless of how close you are, some of them will get new jobs and move on. Friends at church will also come and go at times. When tragedy strikes some of the relationships that you invested heavily in will vanish. One by one, friends in life may disappoint you and let you down. But your spouse will always be by your side. Invest in the one earthly relationship that will remain.

Strong Friendships, Strong Churches

Friendship in a marriage propels your intimacy to new heights and sweetens the journey. Even if the day comes when sex is not a driving factor in your marriage, your friendship will endure and cause your marriage to flourish in wonderful ways. Spouses who struggle to cultivate friendship will find it difficult to experience joy in every other area of their relationship. Marriages fortified by strong friendships impact entire families. I want desperately for my four children to learn to love one another. I want them to experience the joy I had growing up with my brother and sister. I am not saying we didn't fuss at times, but we were friends and we stood up for one another. We prayed for one another and laughed together. I have worked hard to teach my children to be best friends with one another. But how can they do that if Stephanie and I don't show them what a friendship looks like? Strong friendship in marriage will also be a great benefit to the body of Christ.

When you think about it, marriages and families represent some of the primary threads that comprise the fabric of local churches. Dysfunctional marriages do not cultivate the kind of environment at church that guests want to be around. It's pretty obvious when you do not like your spouse enough to treat them with kindness and respect in public. Tension and unresolved bitterness in marriages always spill over into other relationships in the body of Christ. You can't offer the kind of hospitality to your brothers and sisters in Christ if the friendship in your marriage is faltering. But when you foster a deep friendship with your spouse, the community of faith benefits. Your ability to minister to other couples who are hurting will greatly increase as you strengthen your friendship with your spouse. Not only does a friendship sweeten the journey of marriage, it gives you the opportunity to bless your brothers and sisters in Christ.

Homework

1. Discuss what you enjoy doing most together.
2. If you could start a new hobby together, what would it be?
3. Is there anything or anybody who gets in the way of your friendship?
4. What do you cherish most about your friendship?
5. Get creative, think outside the box, and plan a completely new adventure together.
6. Spend time dreaming about the future. What are your goals and ambitions?

A Prayer for You

"Father, thank you for blessing us with a best friend. Thank you for all of the ways you have comforted and ministered to us through each other. Thank you, God, for giving us a companion to share life with.

"Lord, please strengthen our friendship. Help us to treasure our relationship more than any other. Help us to prioritize our friendship by spending lots of time together. Teach us to communicate in ways that strengthen our friendship. Keep us from doing or saying anything to wound our special relationship. Guard our mouths so that we never say hurtful things we cannot take back. Help us to treasure each other. Cultivate a sense of trust between us.

"Keep us from investing in any other relationships that would damage our friendship. Teach us how to support each other when we go through difficult times. 'A friend loves at all times' (Prov. 17:17).

"Help us to find more things that we enjoy doing together. Through every season, help us to cultivate similar interests and pursuits. Help us to have great adventures and make beautiful memories. Help us to be gentle and respectful toward each other even when we don't understand each other. Cause our sex life to flourish in beautiful ways as you strengthen our friendship. May the bond between us grow stronger as we learn to be a better friend to each other. Use our friendship to fortify the bond in our family so that we can strengthen the fellowship in our church.

"You have shown us the greatest love and friendship. 'Greater love has no one than this: to lay down one's life for one's friends' (John 15:13). We are your friend if we do what you command us to do (John 15:14). When we have failed to love each other well, Lord, you are the friend who sticks closer than a brother (Prov. 18:24). May our friendship with you enable us to be refreshing to each other. In Jesus' name, Amen."

Chapter 7

SEX IS THE TRIUMPH OF A PASSIONATE PURSUIT

Scripture Reading: Song of Solomon 7

Remember for a moment that glorious day when you married the love of your life. You stood in front of all your friends and relatives and uttered those words that sealed your marriage. With a nervous and joyous heart, you uttered those two words that you may have thought ended the pursuit of your mate. Although "I do" may have ended your courtship, it did not end your pursuit of your spouse. To the contrary, those words memorialized the beginning of a lifelong pursuit of each other.

Pursuing your spouse probably came naturally before you were married. You called each other constantly. You flirted and exchanged a wide assortment of playful messages. You gladly accepted every inconvenience for the joy of being together. You rearranged your schedules and even traveled out of state just so you could spend more time together. Over time, this zealous pursuit tends to fade in marriage if we are not careful and intentional. One thing is clear, a lackadaisical attitude toward your spouse does not produce the results that Song of Solomon describes. It's easy to take sexual intimacy for granted in marriage. Generally speaking, it can be easy to assume that because you can have sex, the sex will be all that it can be. But marriage is not a time to relax your passionate pursuit.

When you think about it, it's even more important to pursue your spouse after marriage. After marriage we are confronted with a host of issues that we have likely never dealt with. It's after marriage that financial pressures and vocational stress threaten to squash the energy that we used to have for each other. It's after marriage that we are prone to allow the business of raising children to consume the time that we used to spend with each other. If you do not passionately pursue your spouse, there may be temptations to listen to a world that tells us that the marriage covenant does not even matter.

Stop and think about what it must feel like to not be pursued anymore. Your wife is going to feel like she's not treasured or loved anymore. This will introduce a harmful element into your sex life that will ensure her not ever being in the mood. But there are consequences for not pursuing your husband as well. He will feel insignificant and as though he is not being cared for, feelings that will cause a bitter root to grow in his heart. This bitterness may quickly turn to anger and resentment.

Sexual intimacy is the glorious result of having pursued your spouse. It is the glorious head-on collision of two very passionate hearts. If you want to experience the kind of intimacy described in Song of Solomon, you cannot take your spouse for granted. Don't just assume that your spouse is going to desire you. If you take your spouse for granted, there is a good chance that they will take you for granted. Having taken each other for granted, sex cannot possibly be everything that God intended it to be.

The lovers in Song of Solomon recklessly pursue each other. I love how there is nothing lopsided about their pursuit of each other. The only thing that rivals his desire for her is her desire for him. They passionately pursue each other in equal measure. If only one partner is passionate in their pursuit, it will not produce the kind of glorious intimacy that these lovers experience.

What does it look like to pursue your spouse? Let's begin by examining the things she does to pursue her husband.

What Does She Do?

I can hear the objection already: "But women are not supposed to initiate sex!" Says *who?* Where do we get this idea? As I read this book of the Bible devoted to the issue of sexual intimacy, I see a woman who feels incredible freedom to pursue her husband intimately. She is not merely the silent partner who only responds to her husband's advances. Isn't it comical that so many point to the "sexual revolution" of the 1960s as the liberation of a woman to pursue sexual satisfaction? God liberated men and women long ago through the gift of marriage. When it comes to her sexual relationship with her husband, I fail to see any constraints. She is hardly demure in her sexual pursuit of her husband. So let's examine the things that she does to initiate sex with her husband.

She Seduces Him

What she does in pursuing her husband is nothing short of seduction. Everything she says and does helps her lure him in. There is absolutely nothing unholy about seduction between a husband and a wife. On the contrary, Song of Solomon teaches you how to do it.

1. **She makes herself smell good.** She's wearing perfume for the sole purpose of luring him closer. Even during dinner, she's hoping that the aroma will waft in his direction, saying, "While the king was at his table, my perfume spread its fragrance" (1:12). She even beckons the wind to carry her scent toward him, "Awake, north wind, and come, south wind! Blow on my garden, that its fragrance may spread everywhere. Let my beloved come into his garden and taste its choice fruits" (4:16). She goes out of her way to smell good for him, and it works! Her lover adores how she smells and says, "How delightful is your love, my sister, my bride! How much more pleasing is your love than wine, and the fragrance of your perfume more than any spice!" (4:10). Never underestimate the usefulness of a fragrant perfume. The beautiful thing about fragrances is that your husband does not have to

be visually observant to notice. I promise you, your husband will notice that you smell lovely. It's amazing how a distinct fragrance can cement a memory for us. Just one waft of a familiar smell can recall sweet memories from many years ago. What if every time your husband smelled that beautiful aroma, he thought of the last time you made love to him? Smells are absolutely a component of the overall experience of intimacy. If your husband has not bothered to buy you perfume, it might be a great investment.

2. **She talks openly about sex.** It's no secret, men do not always excel when it comes to listening to their wives. Ladies, can I get an amen? But you can help your husband become a better listener by talking about things he cares about. Sex is certainly one of the things that your husband cares deeply about. If you talked about sex half as much as the wife in Song of Solomon, I can assure you his ears would perk nearly every time you opened your mouth. He says, "Show me your face, let me hear your voice; for your voice is sweet, and your face is lovely" (2:14). I promise you, you won't have to talk over the ball game or wait for the commercials to speak if he hears you talking like this woman. Men's hearing gets shamefully selective when the only topics of conversation relate to errands he needs to run, the newest challenges with the kids, or things he needs to fix over the weekend. Let him hear more from you than what's wrong with him, the house, and the kids. Delight his ears and watch them gradually become more attentive to you.

3. **She takes her clothes off.** In what appears to be a dream in chapter 5, she hears her husband knocking at the door. She doesn't get out of bed to come to the door. But she has a good reason. She's naked! She calls from her bed, "I have taken off my robe–must I put it on again? I have washed my feet–must I soil them again?" (5:3). She knows exactly what her husband wants and she gladly offers it to him. If this is not seduction, then I don't know what is! It doesn't take him long at all to respond. In the very next verse, he thrusts his hand forward to open the door (5:4). In marriage,

there is no reason to play cat and mouse. There doesn't have to be any games or playing hard to get. In marriage, you are free to be sexually available for your spouse. And you can do so knowing exactly how he will respond 100 percent of the time. When was the last time you surprised your husband in this manner? This may be difficult for you if you feel self-conscious about the way your body looks. But, remember, although you may not think of your body as ideal, it is the only body that you have to give and the only body that your husband can receive.[1] Your husband married you because he loves you. Trust that God has given your husband an insatiable appetite for how you look. Have you ever considered that he might cherish the very thing that you are most self-conscious about? What you see as an imperfection, he might see as a crown jewel. Don't withhold one of the most precious things that you have to give your husband. Let his eyes feast on you.

4. **She receives his desire.** His desire for his wife doesn't irritate her. She does not make him feel ashamed for desiring her. She does not mock or tease his sexual interest in her. She is so proud of the fact that he desires her in this way. She says, "I belong to my beloved, and his desire is for me" (7:10). She does not want him to set his desire on anybody else. So she revels in his desire and rewards him for it. God made women to want to be desired by their husband. Consider your husband's desire for you a precious gift. Don't make him feel bad for desiring you sexually. Scorn his desire and you will train him to stop desiring you. Out of fear of rejection, he will learn *not* to pursue you. This will be intolerable over time and he will likely grow bitter. Would you rather he set his desire on another woman? Let me be clear: failure on your part does not give your husband a warrant for sinful behavior.

---

1. Gary Thomas, *Sacred Marriage: What If God Designed Marriage to Make Us Holy More Than to Make Us Happy?* (Grand Rapids: Zondervan, 2000), 219.

However, your obedience can encourage obedience in his life. Receive your husband's sexual desire for you with gladness and open arms.

5. **She invites him to make love to her.** Not once, but repeatedly, she beckons him to come and make love to her. In the very beginning of the book, one of the first things out of her mouth is, "Take me away with you–let us hurry! Let the king bring me into his chambers" (1:4). She continues to encourage him throughout the book. In chapter four she invites him, saying, "Let my beloved come into his garden and taste its choice fruits" (4:16). In chapter 7, she invites him yet again: "Let us go early to the vineyards to see if the vines have budded, if their blossoms have opened, and if the pomegranates are in bloom–there I will give you my love" (7:12). She is not waiting for him to ask for sex. She is not waiting for the nagging to be unbearable before she satisfies him. She seeks him out and initiates making love to her husband.

She seduces him and pursues him. Outside of marriage, these are the kinds of behaviors that would render her an immoral woman. Absent marriage, her behavior would make everybody lose respect for her. But within the covenant of marriage, her sexual pursuit of her husband is virtuous. Nobody in their right mind would call her sinful. Her devotion to her husband is obvious to the entire community . . . and they praise her for it.

What about you? Do you initiate sex, or do you always wait for him to ask for it? Do you wait for the hints and flirtatious behavior to reach a feverish pitch before you acquiesce? Or do you surprise your husband with invitations to the bedroom? Don't always wait for your husband to initiate sex. Within the covenant of a marriage relationship, there is no reason to be coy or shy about making love to your husband. Ladies, if you will adopt this same mentality in pursuing your husband, I promise you, your husbands will not object! If you want to see your husband leap and bound across the mountains and over the hills like the husband in Song of Solomon, initiate intimacy (2:8).

This Is What He Does

1. **He talks to her.** Women are generally more verbal than men, so it's no surprise that she has more to say in Song of Solomon. But it is remarkable just how much he *does* say. It's not possible to passionately pursue your spouse if you are not actively communicating your love and affection. Generally speaking, men need to talk to their wives more. If you do not verbally communicate your affection, she will naturally assume that you don't have any. If you do not verbally communicate your attraction, your wife will assume that you are not attracted to her. If you do not let her in on what is going on in your heart, she will imagine the worst. If you cut your wife off from what is going on in your heart, your wife will have no ability to feel close to you. As you pursue your wife, be sure to use words . . . lots of them. Think of the creative use of words as an "inexhaustible well" that you can draw from to "unlock the gateway to intimacy" in your marriage.[2]
2. **He listens to her.** It's not enough to be a talker. You must be a great listener. This is another area where most men have much room for improvement. I will be the first to confess that I don't always do a good job listening. Making your wife feel as though she has been heard is critical. The husband in Song of Solomon listens to his wife and takes his cues from her. His words are evidence that he is paying careful attention to what she is saying. He has heard her say that she does not feel very attractive (1:5–6), so he responds by lavishing compliments on her (4:1–7; 7:1–8). After expressing how ordinary she feels (2:1), he makes sure

2. Gary Smalley and John Trent, *The Language of Love: A Powerful Way to Maximize Insight, Intimacy, and Understanding* (Pomona, CA: Focus on the Family Publishing, 1988), 42.

that she hears him say just how extraordinary she is in his eyes (2:2). She expresses her desire to run away with him, so he essentially says, "Let's go!" (4:8). She invites him to make love to her (4:16), and he does (5:1). He is not only attentive, he begs to hear her voice: "Let me hear your voice" (2:14). Do you know why men have such a hard time with listening? It's work. Listening requires focus and concentration. I know that you are exhausted at the end of a long day, and it's hard for you to pay attention, but your wife needs you to listen. When your wife opens her mouth, it's your job to listen. Don't just listen to what she's saying, pay attention to what she means. Sometimes there is an important distinction between the two.

3. **He holds her.** She describes her husband as having a sculpted muscular body. In her eyes, "His arms are rods of gold set with topaz. His body is like polished ivory" (5:14). With so grand a stature, you would think that she would take delight in his accomplishments. Instead, she celebrates how he uses his strength to hold her. Twice, she says, "His left hand is under my head, and his right arm embraces me" (2:6; 8:3). With so many other erotic things going on in Song of Solomon, why would she boast of how he holds her? The answer can only be that she wanted to be held. She needed to be held. Don't ever underestimate the impact of simply holding your wife. What good are your muscles if you don't use them to embrace your wife? Your wife absolutely wants to be held. When you embrace your wife, she feels loved and secure. When you hold her, she feels as though everything is going to be okay. Though you might tend to minimize the value of a simple embrace, your wife does not.

4. **He invites her to come away.** Over and over in the book of Song of Solomon, we have this refrain, "Come away with me." They are not leaving to go sightsee or to visit relatives. Every time you hear this refrain in the book, it signals a need to get away from everything in order to focus their time and energy on loving each other sexually. These lovers have a pressing need to demon-

strate their love for each other. Think about this for a moment. Sexual intimacy is so important that it is deserving of the highest priority in your marriage. So important, in fact, that you may need to leave town in order to focus your time and energy on it. That's right! It may be time in your marriage to pack your bags and plan a trip. Take a vacation and get away with your lover. Ask for time off, get a babysitter, book your flight for a cruise, and go! It may seem expensive, but I can assure you it's far less expensive than a messy divorce. You travel for your job; is your marriage any less important? It may seem crazy to give this much attention to sexual intimacy, but the lack of attention is precisely what causes problems in marriages. Ignore this side of your marriage, and you will not be unscathed for long. Just because you may not be thinking about this area of your marriage does not mean that your partner is not silently suffering. Inattention to this component of your marriage has the potential of causing all kinds of problems.

5. **He adorns her with jewelry.** I have never really understood the usefulness of jewelry in a marriage. Aside from an engagement ring, aren't husbands pretty much done with jewelry? For most husbands, the expense does not make much sense. If it's about being thoughtful, there are so many less expensive ways to show my care for her. If it is merely about owning something beautiful, I can think of so many other more practical things that are equally beautiful. But neither of these sentiments are the motivation for jewelry in Song of Solomon. The point of the jewelry is not the jewelry itself. It's not as though this woman is craving beautiful shiny things for herself. He longs to adorn her with jewelry because her beauty is deserving of it. He's not showing off his ability to purchase expensive things; he is showing off his wife! He buys her jewelry because he is so proud of her. As he contemplates her beauty, he longs to decorate her: "Your cheeks are beautiful with earrings, your neck with strings of jewels. We will make you earrings of gold, studded with silver" (1:10–11).

Think about it: we have a tendency to decorate things that we are proud of. We hang décor and put up Christmas decorations to accentuate the beauty of our home. We hang pictures on the wall because we are thankful to have a nice home. We dress our children in nice clothes because we want the world to appreciate how great they are. When the husband in Song of Solomon sees his wife, he sees a magnificent beauty that demands adornment. When is the last time you gave your wife jewelry? It does not have to be dripping with diamonds or sapphires. In fact, it doesn't even have to be very expensive at all. Your thoughtful gift will communicate how beautiful your wife is in your eyes. A gift of jewelry will be worth its weight in gold. Lavish flattery will certainly warrant the best kind of thank you!

A Recipe for Killing Your Pursuit

Every relationship is different, but there are some things that have a nearly universal ability to throw cold water on the kind of passionate pursuit that we see in Song of Solomon. If you want to throw cold water on your spouse, here are four great ways to do it. Follow these four easy steps, and I guarantee you will forever keep wild passion from your marriage. In no time at all, you are sure to see your sex life diminish into a mere afterthought.

1. **Watch an excessive amount of television every night.** If both of you watch your own favorite TV show every night of the week, this does not leave very much time for intimacy. By the time you have completed all of your obligations for the day and cleaned up the dinner dishes, you will have precious little time to spend together. Do you really want to squander this time by staring at a screen? Television has a strange way of sedating you. You are not likely to have the kind of energy that these lovers in Song of Solomon have for each other if you spend too much time watching TV.

I think it's great to relax by watching a show together. Sometimes, at the end of a long day, it can be a nice way to unwind. But you might consider limiting your screen time so that you can interact with each other in meaningful ways. I recommend laughing and talking together. Spend time reminiscing and dreaming about the future. Talk about your day and share your burdens with each other. Interacting with each other will fuel your pursuit of each other and lead to more intimacy.

2. **Be a workaholic.** There will always be sacrifices when it comes to providing well for your family. There may be many occasions when you are forced to work late in order to put food on the table and achieve your vocational goals. But if you do not make time for your spouse, you are not likely to experience the kind of amazing passion that you read about in Song of Solomon.

Try hard to come home at a reasonable hour in the evening. It's your responsibility to know when to stop for the day. If you have given an honest day's work, go home and be with your spouse. Work as efficiently as you can while you are at the office so that you can come home at a reasonable hour. Do your best to move as many meetings as you can within the boundaries of normal working hours. Working hard and setting an example for other employees is a good thing. But if your marriage is compromised, you could reach the point where you are no longer any good to your employer. It is in their best interest for you to draw healthy boundaries. God will honor your heart to be a good husband or good wife. Work hard at your job, but do not sacrifice what is most important in order to make money.

Remember, pursuing your spouse takes a lot of effort. Work at pursuing your spouse. Save your best energy for pursuing each other. If you don't invest energy into pursuing your mate, you will not get to reap the harvest of intimacy. Intimacy follows your passionate pursuit of one another.

3. **Put yourself first.** A great way to stifle the sexual energy in your relationship is to think exclusively about yourself. From the moment you wake up in the morning, forget your spouse and think about what you want to do, how you want to do it, and when you want to do it. Try your best to cater in any way, shape, or form to your needs, wants, and desires. Talk about yourself incessantly and require your spouse

to do everything that you want them to do, with total disregard for their needs and desires. Structure every day around yourself and do not do anything that would in any way seem selfless or sacrificial for your spouse. Avoid even the appearance of inconveniencing yourself to support or encourage your spouse. Be diligent in assuming that literally everything in your house will revolve around you.

Selfishness has a devastating effect on every relationship in your life. Selfishness has no place within the selfless paradigm of marriage. Marriage is all about putting your spouse first. It's your job to lay down your preferences for the good of your marriage. God is calling you to sacrificially love your spouse. God wants you to die to yourself and wash the feet of your spouse.

The more you put your spouse first, the more they will put you first. Your spouse will be more available for you sexually if they see a servant's heart in you. What can you do today to minister to your spouse? The more you do for your spouse, the more time and energy they will have to pursue you. Live life putting your spouse first and enjoy the benefits of them putting you first. A glorious collision takes place when both husband and wife rush to put each other first.

4. **Hang out with your friends . . . a lot.** Having close friendships is such a blessing in life. We all need time to cultivate meaningful relationships. If you invest in the right relationships in the right ways, God will help you grow into the strong Christian He wants you to be. But if you find yourself spending every other weekend hanging out with the guys, it will be hard to experience the kind of passion in Song of Solomon. Ladies, if you are always being whisked away by your friends to go shopping, don't be surprised if your husband starts acting cold toward you. Invest yourself in meaningful relationships. Work hard at being a good friend to those who have always been there for you. But remember that the most precious relationship in your life is with your spouse.

It's not possible to passionately pursue your spouse when you are not making your partner a real priority in your life. The lovers in

Song of Solomon are not accidentally finding themselves embroiled in a fantastic sex life. They have set their sights on each other and have determined to run with abandon toward each other. When your passionate pursuit of each other is successful, you will experience the sensational collision that these two lovers experience. Absent an intentional pursuit of your spouse, you will experience your sex life drifting into established ruts of status quo. If, however, you are ready to experience new heights in your love life, work on passionately pursuing your spouse. Don't ever let your pursuit of each other diminish.

Great love always pursues. Is this not the story of the Bible? After centuries of wandering, God still pursued His people. The Lord pledged in Ezekiel 34:11, "I myself will search for my sheep and look after them." The psalmist in Psalm 119 beckons the Lord to seek him in his wandering (119:176). This is the also the story of the gospel. When you were sinful and unworthy, God pursued you with His love. "But God demonstrates his own love for us in this: While we were still sinners, Christ died for us" (Rom. 5:8). After coming to faith in Christ, He continues to pursue a more intimate relationship with you. Love always pursues! Aren't you glad that God never stops pursuing you? His constant pursuit of you is evidence of the fact that He loves you. You can show the love of Christ to your spouse by always pursuing a closer relationship with them.

Homework

1. Describe to each other a time in your relationship when you aggressively pursued each other. What kinds of things did you do then that you don't do as much anymore?
2. Answer the following question for each other. "How do you want to be pursued?"
3. Take turns finishing the following sentence, "After reading this chapter, I think I could do a better job . . ."
4. On your own, spend time plotting a strategy for how you are going to pursue your spouse this week.

A Prayer for You

"Father, thank you for pursuing me with your love and grace when I was dead in my sin. Thank you for wooing me by your Holy Spirit! Thank you for loving and pursuing me even when I was not loveable. I love you because you first loved me. Your love for me is evident through the gracious gift of a spouse.

"You love and care for me daily through the precious gift of marriage. Help us to respond in gratitude by continuing to pursue each other.

"We confess that we have taken each other for granted and have failed at times to pursue each other in the ways we need to. The safety of our marriage covenant has left us careless of each other. Though lax in our pursuit of each other, we have intensely pursued so many other things of lesser importance. Help us not to chase the vain things of this world and neglect the most important relationship in our life.

"Father, help us to vigilantly pursue a closer relationship with you so that we will be careful to lovingly pursue each other as well. Help us to leverage our time, energy, and resources to draw nearer to each other. Help us both to understand the ways in which the other wants and needs to be pursued. Give us both a sensitivity to each other that we don't naturally have. Through our words and our actions, help us continue to chase each other. Help us never to grow complacent about each other. Guard us from the kinds of activities that will diminish our pursuit of you and each other. Keep us from selfishness and empty habits that steal our time away from you and each other. Keep our daily obligations from squandering the precious time that we have to spend with each other. Cause our sexual intimacy to flourish as we zealously pursue a closer relationship.

"As we pursue each other more passionately, strengthen our marriage against the Enemy's plots. May our pursuit of each other result in a stronger marriage and a greater impact on a lost world. Use the example of our marriage to heal many other marriages. In Jesus' name, Amen."

Chapter 8

SEX IS FEASTING

Scripture Reading: Song of Solomon 8

What in the world does food have to do with sex? Great question! Song of Solomon is saturated with references to eating and drinking. From the very beginning of the book, their love is said to be "more delightful than wine."[1] She compares her lover to an apple tree in the forest, whose fruit is sweet (2:3). She thinks of his cheeks as beds of spice (5:13). He reciprocates by referring to her temples as "halves of a pomegranate" (4:3) and by associating her with the most fragrant of spices (4:14). Her breasts are like "clusters of fruit" (7:7). Making love to her is like feasting on honeycomb, milk, and honey (5:1). She longs for her husband to take her into the banquet house. But the association of food and sex is actually not unique to Song of Solomon.

In the book of Proverbs, we find several verses that interrelate food and sex. The adulterous woman in Proverbs 30 "eats and wipes her mouth and says, 'I've done nothing wrong'" (v. 20). The young man in Proverbs 5 is warned against tasting the honey dripping from the

1. References to wine include 1:2, 4; 4:10; 5:1; 7:2, 9; 8:2.

mouth of the adulterous woman (v. 3). Instead, men are encouraged to be satisfied and intoxicated with their wives (Prov. 5:18–19). In Proverbs 9, the woman named Folly entices those who pass by to enjoy a secret feast at her home: a not-so-subtle reference to adultery.[2] We also see the intermingling of sex and food in Exodus 32 at the Golden Calf incident where the people ate, then got up to "play," a verb that likely includes sexual overtones.[3] It's also interesting to note that the union between Christ and His Bride (the Church) will be enjoyed at the wedding supper of the Lamb (Rev. 19:9). Over and over, we see this intertwining metaphor of food and intimacy.

Let's explore this metaphor of feasting to see what we might learn about sexual intimacy in marriage.

Hunger. Every great feast begins with a powerful appetite. The greater the appetite, the more you will enjoy a feast. There is such a predictable cycle when it comes to our physical hunger. We eat, we are satisfied, then we are hungry again. No matter how well you have eaten, your appetite will always return. What better way to convey the sexual appetite that we should have for our lover? The appetite you have for your spouse always returns, regardless of how many times

---

2. Garrett, *Proverbs*, 116. The seriousness of the sin is evident in the fact that those who oblige the woman's folly end up in the realm of the dead (Prov. 9:18).

3. The Hebrew verb translated "to indulge in revelry" is used in contexts that include sexual connotations. Potipher's wife accuses Joseph of sexually assaulting her using the same verb (Gen. 39:14, 17). The Philistines discovered that Rebekah was Isaac's wife because he was "playing" with her (Gen. 26:8). In his discussion of Paul's reference to Exodus 32, Fee also maintains an erotic sense of the Hebrew verb because of Genesis 26:8. As Fee notes, the association of sexual activity and eating in Exodus 32 is consistent with the story of Numbers 25:1–3, where the Israelites are clearly engaging in both sexual immorality and participation in pagan feasting. See Gordon D. Fee, *The First Epistle to the Corinthians,* The New International Commentary on the New Testament (Grand Rapids: Wm. B. Eerdmans, 1987), 454. However, Stuart claims, "If any overtone of sexual debauchery is intended here, it is not followed through in the rest of the narrative . . ." But you could interpret the lack of additional information as unnecessary if indeed the word includes a sexual sense. See Douglas Stuart, *Exodus: An Exegetical and Theological Exposition of Holy Scripture,* The New American Commentary (Nashville: Broadman and Holman, 2006), 666. See also Revelation 2:14.

you have feasted on each other. It's like filling a bucket that has a hole in the bottom. Even if you fill the bucket to overflowing, it will be empty soon. In fact, from the moment you fill the bucket, it immediately starts leaking. The leak in the bucket is not a design flaw, but the genius of the designer. The God-given hunger keeps husbands and wives drawn to each other in a way that strengthens and unifies. No matter what, your spouse will always be getting hungry. Feed them. If you are struggling to cultivate or maintain a sexual appetite for your spouse, now might be a good time to skip ahead to the appendix to read about how you can manage this issue in your marriage.

Food. Their bodies provide the perfect nourishment for their sexual needs. Only food can quell a physical hunger, and only sex can fulfil a sexual hunger. Your spouse has the kind of food that no other person on the planet can offer you. Your spouse is one of a kind. Nowhere on the planet can you find the kind of delicacies that they have to offer you. This is not just any kind of feast, but the best kind. It's a feast comprised only of dessert. No forcing down kale at this meal to get to the good part. This is the kind of meal that you never want to rush through. The kind of meal that will help you burn calories instead of consume them. You can put the silverware down too. This meal you are free to enjoy with your hands. But remember: wonderful feasts also require preparation.

Preparations. A wonderful banquet is never an afterthought. A vast array of preparations will accompany any great feast. Banquets don't just happen; they are the product of a lot of hard work. If you doubt me, simply inform your wife that you have invited your boss over for dinner tonight and watch her reaction (from a safe distance). A banquet usually begins with making a list of everything you will need for the meal. Then you go to the store. Sometimes you even make multiple trips. After purchasing everything you will need to feed your guests, you then begin the laborious process of cooking. You get out your cookbooks and slowly begin the process of sautéing, mixing, seasoning, and garnishing. A good host also thinks about how to make all of the guests feel welcome, loved, and honored. Where will your guests park, and which entrance will they use to enter your home? Where will they sit at the dinner table, and which plates will you use? Will you have music playing in the background? When it comes to a banquet, the presentation of the food is every bit as important as the food itself. Careful planning has gone into how the food looks. Grand feasts are never an afterthought!

Sex with your spouse should not be merely an afterthought either (though if there ever was an afterthought worth having . . .). If you wait until 10:30 p.m. to start thinking about providing your spouse a feast, you may end up only providing a quick snack. Don't get me wrong: snacks can be a great idea! You may not always have time for a feast. But the question is, what can you do to make sure sex is special for your spouse? Even the smallest amount of thoughtful preparation can make intimacy so nourishing at the end of a long day.

Husbands are notoriously bad at helping to prepare their wives for intimacy. Just because you can go from zero to 90 in 0.2 seconds (on a slow day) does not mean that your wife can do the same. Be sensitive to her needs and do what you can so that she is ready for you in the evening. When was the last time you wrote a poem for her? Maybe you could cook for her and even do the dishes while she enjoys a relaxing bath. When was the last time you arranged for a babysitter and surprised your wife with a romantic date? What can you do to make your wife feel relaxed? Maybe you could give her a few minutes alone with her favorite book and some soft music. One of the best things that you can do to prepare her for a banquet is simply spend time with her. Can you leave work a little bit early? Your wife is not ready to feast if she has not connected with you. While you may think of sex as a connecting of sorts, I can promise you that she has something very different in mind. Sit down, take a deep breath, and ask her about her day. Let her talk about everything that's bothering her. Let her talk about every frustrating thing that happened in her day. Maybe you could stop by the store and pick up some flowers or some other thoughtful gift that you know she would love. Help her get the kids in bed so that she will have plenty of time and energy. Select her favorite music and set the lighting. Do everything you can to make the ambience as relaxing and peaceful as possible. Even the smallest thoughtful preparation can reap satisfying dividends.

Wives, just because your husband is always willing and ready to "pig out" at the drop of a hat doesn't mean that you can't do something more to make intimacy special for him. Given that your husband is visual, maybe you could wear something you know that he will like. Is there an "hors d'oeuvres" you could feed him before he leaves for work? Maybe you could send him a tantalizing message of what is on the menu for tonight. When he gets home from work, maybe you could greet him in a way that will make him grow weak in the knees. Maybe you could simplify dinner or just order out so that you can get on to the more important meal. When it comes to sex, do not forget the important preparations that will make his meal special. Don't take sex for granted; work hard to prepare a feast. With such grand preparations being made, there is sure to be a mounting anticipation for the feast.

Anticipation. The mere aroma of a feast can make us salivate. I love smelling fresh baked bread, Indian curries, apple pie, and cookies. My favorite time of year is Thanksgiving. An entire day nearly is spent waiting for the big feast: a feast which never disappoints.

In much the same way, I sense a lot of anticipation between these two lovers in Song of Solomon. They long and desire for each other. They literally cannot stop thinking and talking about each other. They are consumed with glorious concern for each other. With great anticipation, she daydreams about sitting underneath his shade to taste his fruit (2:3). Meanwhile, he's thinking about climbing her stature to take hold of her breasts (7:7–8).

Most husbands will excel when it comes to cultivating a sexual appetite for their wives. Normally, they will have no difficulty at all focusing on the evening's activities throughout the day. Whatever distraction is hindering you, believe me, it will pass and you'll be back on track. But wives may have to be more intentional in this area. You may have to cultivate an appetite for intimacy by intentionally thinking about being with your husband at various points throughout the day. Pray for him throughout the day. Think about the first time he kissed you. Remember the first time he held your hand and how it made your stomach flip. Daydream about your first date and how special he made you feel. Reread that last love note he gave you on your anniversary.

Indulging. In a fine banquet, the host would never dream of monitoring the guests' portions. To the contrary, the host labors to make sure every guest knows that there is freedom to eat to their heart's content. Remember, there are only two guests at this feast. It's clear in Song of Solomon that the husband is not "eating with moderation" when it comes to his wife. He's not rationing the food or fasting. Instead, he is feasting and indulging in every delicacy that she has to offer. There is no need to exercise self-control when it comes to feasting on his wife. And unlike indulging on food, there are no downsides to a sexual feast. He's not going to get sick to his stomach as he might if he were to overeat. He's not going to suffer from heartburn or indigestion. When it comes to real food, we always regret overindulging. In fact, our feast sometimes leads to fresh intentions of dieting in the days to come. But a sexual feast between a husband and wife leaves no residue of regret. Instead, their feasting leads to a deep satisfaction.

She allows him to explore her entire body. The wife withholds nothing from her lover. She gives him unfettered access to herself. She gives him the freedom to enjoy all of who God made her to be, and she enjoys the same privilege with him. She invites him to make love to her and gives him all of the time he needs. And their feasting lasts all night! She compares her lover to a deer who spends the night browsing among the lilies (2:16–17).

My wife and I stayed in the mountains of northern Georgia several weeks ago. Nestled into six mountains was a sprawling planned community filled with cabins and fun things to do. The one thing I did not see in this resort community was landscaping. Even in front of the most magnificent homes, all we saw were trees. Normally, million-dollar homes have perfectly manicured landscaping filled with all different colors, textures, and levels of flourishing flowers and bushes. The closest I came to seeing that, however, was an occasional lonely bush surrounded by a cage meant to keep the deer from devouring it. Planting flowers and bushes was completely pointless because of all of the deer. The mountains were crawling with hungry deer foraging for substance. But imagine a hungry deer, weary of scavenging for acorns and nuts, discovering a flourishing vineyard filled with succulent plants of the rarest and most delicious varieties. Well, this is exactly what her husband has discovered in his wife. Upon finding his bride, he stays all night, devouring everything in sight. His wife provides for him an "all you can eat" buffet. With so many delights to enjoy, there is no possibility of sleep. He takes his time and consumes everything available to him.

But if we are going to think through this metaphor of feasting, we need to think about what happens when a person does not eat enough.

When it comes to physical food, those who have not eaten properly can experience a number of symptoms that range from mild to severe. Everything from mild dizziness and difficulty concentrating to severe pain can come as a result of not eating. It is not pressing the metaphor too far to say that the lack of sex in some marriages is causing deep and lasting problems. Yes, people can grow irritable and have difficulty concentrating if it has been too long. In some cases, resentment and bitterness turn to anger when couples do not have a healthy sex life. Don't think for a moment that your marriage can remain unscathed by neglecting each other's sexual needs. But the goal is not to give just enough "food" for your spouse. God wants you to provide a feast.

Is your bedroom a banquet hall? If not, it needs to be. Not a snack bar or a place to throw down a few finger foods. It's not a convenience store with only the lowest quality nourishment to offer. It's not a place for warmed-over leftovers or cheap frozen foods. A banquet suggests a feast where the food never runs out. A banquet means that you provide wondrous delicacies for your spouse. It means giving your spouse the very best and encouraging them to indulge to their heart's content. A banquet means gladly catering to the holy appetites of your spouse. The difficulty in most marriages pertains to the issue of how the feast is provided. So let's dive into this issue and see if we can work to understand how men and women think differently.

Understanding Your Husband

"You want to do it again?" As the evening gradually fades into night, the subtle hints grow stronger and stronger by the minute. But as the sexual overtones fail to achieve the intended results, the hints become eclipsed by more overt gestures. Exhausted by the day's flurry of activity, your hair still in a messy bun, you look down at your flannel pajamas from circa 1984 laden with an untold number of unidentified splotches and spills from the children, trying desperately to understand what may have got him going. With sincere exasperation you ask him the same question that always elicits the same response, "You want to do it again?"

For the wives who have asked this question many times, by now you should know that the answer will always be "yes, yes, and more yes." This answer is as predictable as your need for air and water. As surely as you will never refuse chocolate, he will always desire sex. It's as predictable as the rising of the tide. As the sun rises and sets predictably every day, so his answer will *always* be "yes, yes, and more yes."

His desire to have sex again might be puzzling to you after you've already enjoyed one or more great experiences that week. However, in his mind, those experiences, while wonderful, are a distant memory. Things in the rearview mirror sometimes appear more distant than they really are. In fact, those great experiences heighten his awareness of how long it's been. Take heart, it's not that you failed to satisfy him, but that you have *succeeded* in satisfying him. So successful, in fact, that he cannot stop thinking about it. Hours feel like days and days feel like months for him. Even if it's only been a day, a husband can feel as though he's been wandering around in a barren wilderness for twenty-four hours, desperate for sustenance. In a state like this, it takes little provocation or no provocation at all to get him going.

"I feel like we are needing two very different things right now." Let's face it, you are needy person. Not only are you a needy person, but you married a needy person. Sometimes you and your spouse will share the same need at the same time, but oftentimes your needs will be very different. When your needs don't complement each other, sometimes you will find yourself arguing. When it comes to sex, this is often the case. What should you do?

The first thing you need to know is that his needs are just as legitimate as yours. Second, you don't necessarily have to choose between whose needs get met. Wives, if your husband has met your need with such kind sensitivity, then it's your turn to meet his need with the same measure of love and care. Neither one of you has the right to say that your need is more important than your spouse's needs. Before the day is done, lovingly meet each other's needs.

"Sometimes it's difficult to focus on anything else." If it has been a while since you have had sex, it can be difficult for him to focus on anything but making love to you. Every time he sets his mind to a task, his mind will drift back to you with a mighty longing that can scarcely be put into words. It's not terrible for him to feel this way from time to time, but it's also not healthy to remain in this state too long. There is simply too much sexual temptation in this world for your husband to struggle in a state of sexual urgency. There is definitely an upside for you in the way that God hardwired your husband. He literally cannot stop thinking about you. He can't wait to hold you and touch you. He longs to caress you and make love to you. He desires you so deeply that he struggles to think of anything else. This is the kind of desire you want to stoke in your marriage.

"Why does it always have to lead to sex?" Even the most innocuous physical contact can bring your husband to a frenzy. After a long hug or a simple kiss before bedtime, you may have found yourself asking the same question that many millions of women have asked their husbands, "Why does it always have to lead to sex?" It's ironic that, as many times as men have heard this question, they have not once understood it. From the woman's perspective, there is a longing for physical intimacy that does not have to include sex. For a woman, there are so many moments where a nonsexual embrace is more than enough. From the husband's standpoint, this is like bringing a succulent piece of meat three inches from your mouth, only to set it back on the plate again. Or, to use a different metaphor, it would be like watching a long movie and never getting to see the long-awaited climactic ending. So in answer to the question "Why does it always have to lead to sex?" the husband would respond, saying, "Because it *can* lead to sex!" The question he's asking is, "Why wouldn't you want it to lead to sex?" At the root of this misunderstanding between men and women is a fundamental difference in needs.

Three Important Issues for Men

When it comes to real estate, they say that there are three critically important issues: location, location, location. Obviously, this is a gross overstatement that serves to heighten the importance of location. Naturally, the size, type, and quality of construction are also very important. However, even a home lacking optimal construction can be worth top dollar if the location is right. People will compromise on so many things if it means living in the right neighborhood. When it comes to sexual intimacy, there are three important things in a man's mind: frequency, frequency, frequency. Naturally, a man cares about other things as well when it comes to sex. But in general, they don't matter as much if the frequency is lacking.

This absolutely does not mean that you must have sex every time he wants it. But, please, know this! Improving the frequency of sex in your marriage is probably the simplest solution to improving your sex life in the mind of your husband. In fact, if you are ever at a loss as to how to satisfy your husband in the bedroom, start with improving the frequency of sex. Change nothing else about your sex life, and I promise you that he will observe an incredible improvement in the bedroom.

God Made Your Husband This Way

Yes, your husband thinks differently about sex, and that is okay.

God has hardwired your husband to desire sex because it accomplishes his goal of being fruitful and multiplying. Sexual intimacy also helps your husband pay attention to you. Your husband's desire is not unhealthy or evidence that he has been tainted by a sexually saturated world. His desire for you is not a consequence of the Fall in Genesis 3, but evidence of God's handiwork. Though you may feel frustrated with your husband's inexhaustible desire for intimacy, it would not be in your best interests for him to feel indifferent about it. It's to your benefit to have a husband who fawns over you every day of your life. Do you really want a husband who scarcely looks your direction? Deep in your heart you want his endless attraction and affection. Your marriage would be stale and lonely if he did not earnestly want to make love to you. In your frustration with his sexual desire, be sure that you don't fault the way God made your husband.

Extended physical contact without sex is difficult. A man's sexual needs make it very difficult at times to have extended and loving physical contact with his wife without the added pleasure of intercourse. You may be able to watch a long movie while holding your husband without any desire to have sex afterwards, but your husband can't. In fact, it can actually lead to physical discomfort for him, especially if it has been a while since your last sexual encounter. Your husband will find it very difficult to put the brakes on after spending a lot of time holding and caressing you. When it comes to long moments of physical contact, it's never nonsexual for your husband. In fact, a man has a tendency to view every hug, kiss, and flirtatious glance as a prelude to something much better.

What hinders you does not hinder him. When you see that special glimmer in his eyes, you might be flabbergasted that your husband could even think about sex "at a time like this." The things that hinder you from desiring intimacy do nothing to restrain your husband's sexual desire. Let's consider a few things that will do nothing to stifle your husband.

Routine fatigue and exhaustion do not hinder your husband. For many women, sex feels like a chore at the end of a long exhausting day. For your husband, sex is the perfect ending to an exhausting day. It's the cherry on top, no matter how his day went. Regardless of how tired he is, he will usually have just enough energy to end the day well. Your husband does not think about sex as a draining task; instead, it's a way for him to release stress and fatigue.

Clearly, there are going to be moments when he doesn't have the energy, but generally speaking, you can count on him being ready. After completing his first Iron Man competition, he will have plenty of energy for sex. After finishing his first ascent of El Capitan or having suffered a bruising defeat in his latest midlife Jujitsu phase, he will have conserved more than enough energy for you.

Even illness may be no match for his sexual desire for you. Chances are, whatever kept him home from work will not keep him from you. Headaches? No problem. Allergies? Not an issue. Common cold? Piece of cake. Even aches and pains that kept him from working in the yard will miraculously subside long enough for him to take care of business. Only serious illness can debilitate him when it comes to sex.

Don't think for a moment that a dirty house will hinder his desire. Dirty dishes and piled laundry are just great examples of things that can absolutely wait. The long list of things that might hinder your focus easily fade behind what he considers to be the more important task of making love to you. Frankly, it does not matter how busy he is, I can assure you he always has time for one more thing.

If you are a list person, let me put it to you this way: he wakes up nearly every day of his life with you at the tippy top of his list. On the rare occasion that he does not wake up with this at the top of this list, it only takes about a split second for that to change. No joke!

You should also know that he has no need to feel attractive to be in the mood. When his hair is nappy and he's badly in need of a shower, he feels like the timing is perfect. (In fact, if you fall into that same category . . . still, no problem). Whereas your desire might rise and fall based upon how you feel about yourself, I can assure you that he's not thinking about whether he feels attractive at the moment. He's not worried about how bloated he feels or about how many Cheetos he consumed over lunch. He's not stressed about you thinking that he's let his body go. Nor is he regretting the third jelly-filled donut. In fact, he might feel very good about that jelly donut. He's not thinking about any of those things that sometimes distract you from making love. He's thinking about you!

He's Counting on It

In chapter 7 of Song of Solomon, the wife promises to make love to her husband, saying, "There I will give you my love" (v. 12). But she doesn't just say it, she follows through. When it comes to sexual intimacy, follow-through is critically important. When you hint at making love to your husband, your words leave an indelible impression on his mind. Your words become etched in stone, so to speak, on the heart of your husband. Every moment that follows is lived in anticipation of making love to you. Right or wrong, your husband is so thrilled with the idea that it's all he can think about the rest of the day.

Then, life happens. It's not that you didn't mean the words when you said them, but the busyness and chaos of life sometimes take over. All of a sudden, you're thinking about every unfinished task staring you in the face. You feel anything but sexy when you look at the piles of dirty laundry, dirty dishes, and children who need to be bathed and put to bed. Whereas your husband is blissfully unaware of the change in your countenance and is still clinging to the assurance that his day is going to end very well. Meanwhile, you assume that your husband is sensitive enough to know that there is no possibility that you are still in the mood. It's at this point that sparks begin to fly, and they're not the kind that he was hoping for.

So what can be done?

Maybe you can express your desire for him in a way that does not give him false expectations. Maybe you could say something along the lines of "Honey, I want you to know that I really desire you tonight, so let's try to make that happen if it's possible." This will help you communicate your desire for your husband in a manner that is less likely to lead to conflict. There is also something to be said for following through with sex even if you are not as into it as you were at the beginning of the day.

Just because you are not able to capture how you hoped to make love to your husband does not mean that it cannot be incredibly meaningful to him. If you do not have the energy to create the ambience and the mood that you wanted, no worries. You can still make the day end very well for your husband. Is your desire to not have sex so strong that you are willing to argue about it for twenty minutes? And how does that make sense when you could've satisfied him in half that time?

Yes, sometimes life makes it nearly impossible to follow through with your word. But it's not very nice to say one thing and then do the complete opposite. It is in your best interests for your word to mean something to him. How would you feel if he promised to spend the day with you, then, at the last minute, decided that he was not in the mood anymore? Would it make you feel any better if he told you that the day did not go as he expected? The Bible says, "Hope deferred makes the heart sick, but a longing fulfilled is a tree of life" (Prov. 13:12). You get to choose between that which makes him sick and that which gives life.

"I just feel like I have not connected with you." If you have said it once, you have said it countless times. You know exactly what you mean when you say this to your husband. But here's what you might not know. Sex helps your husband remain emotionally connected. Making love to your husband will help him meet your emotional needs. According to Slattery, "The lack of regular sex is a significant barrier to emotional connectedness and intimacy for men. Likewise, sex is perhaps the most powerful force bonding a man emotionally and relationally to his wife. Beyond just the act of having sex, sharing and embracing your husband's sexuality is perhaps the most powerful way to build the intimacy you so desire in your marriage."[4]

Do you see how masterfully God works through the gift of sexual intimacy? A wife positions the husband to give her what she needs by giving him what he needs. As Linda Dillow notes, "When you make love to your husband, you touch his soul and create an outlet of expression for his emotions."[5] By fulfilling his sexual needs, you enable him to meet your emotional needs. It is in your best interests to make love to your husband.

"Not Gonna Happen." If you are in no condition to make love to your husband, then communicate this to your husband with gentleness and grace. I think you can do better than "It's not gonna happen." If you are harsh with your words or tone, it will seem cruel and he will struggle with resentment. Remember that his "crime" is desiring you. He loves you and thinks you are beautiful. This is hardly the kind of egregious offense that should solicit a sharp remark from you. So choose your words carefully and strive to be gentle. The Bible teaches that "A gentle answer turns away wrath, but a harsh word stirs up anger" (Prov. 15:1). You might also think about making plans for the next day, saying, "Honey, let's wake up early in the morning" or "Can you come home early for lunch?" will go a long way with your husband. Say "no" in a way that communicates your desire to be with him sexually at some other moment in the near future. In fact, it might even intensify your intimacy at the next available opportunity if you have this to look forward to.

It Feels Hurtful

I know that this is going to sound really strange, but you really need to hear this. If your husband feels like you are uninterested in him

---

4. https://www.focusonthefamily.com/marriage/sex-and-intimacy/understanding-your-husbands-sexual-needs/sex-is-a-relational-need.
5. Linda Dillow and Lorraine Pintus, *Intimate Issues: Conversations Woman to Woman* (Colorado Springs: Waterbrook Press, 2000), 41.

sexually, all of the nonsexual affection seems hurtful and patronizing to him. It's hurtful in the sense that it feels taunting if it never leads to intercourse. He would much rather not get excited than get excited with no outlet. For the sake of your marriage, he will pull away from you, not wanting to be wound up in a world where he will face temptation. It may also seem patronizing, because the nonsexual affection does not seem flattering or affectionate if there is only rarely an opportunity to make love. If he feels like there is no possibility of it leading to sex, the hugs, kisses, and hand-holding feel like a burden. Without sex, he has a hard time receiving affection, because ultimately he's thinking, "But you don't really want me because if you did, you would want to make love to me." Instinctively, he will disengage from you emotionally and in every other way.

Understanding Your Wife

God made your wife this way. God made your wife just the way He wanted her. Don't assume that because she is different, she is in the wrong. Don't spend your precious time together complaining about these differences. She is "fearfully and wonderfully made" (Ps. 139:14). God did not want her to be just like you. It's your job to acknowledge the beauty of those differences and to thank God for them. Instead of trying to change her, ask God how He might want you to change. Admire your wife for whom God made her to be. Relish every opportunity to deepen your relationship with her through the kinds of nonsexual intimacy that she desires. Do your best to understand how these differences cultivate a much stronger partnership as you serve the Lord together. Think about all of the ways her strengths complement your weaknesses. Yes, she does not think about sexual intimacy in the very same way, and that is okay. Love your wife for who God made her to be.

Flirting doesn't always mean sex. When your wife flirts with you, it could mean many things. I realize that you only mean one thing when you flirt with her, but she's not like you; she's a woman! Flirting could mean she's enjoying your company. It could mean she wants to feel close to you. She might mean that she thinks you're handsome. She could be saying she loves you. She might just be in the mood to flirt. There are probably seventeen or more things she could possibly mean. When she flirts with you, do not make the mistake of assuming she's promising you sex that night. Let your wife be playful without making her feel bad for not making love to you.

"Can't we just cuddle?" Your wife longs for nonsexual affection. Don't get me wrong, she absolutely needs you sexually as well. But your wife has a need to feel loved in a way that has nothing to do with your sexual needs. She has a need to feel like she is appreciated for who she is as a person and not simply what she can provide for you sexually. She longs to feel connected to you emotionally. She needs to hear you say that you love her and not just the sex. She wants to feel like more than just your sexual outlet. She wants to be your best friend. She wants to enjoy your company without anything being required of her. She wants you to hold her hand and spend time with her. She longs to share her thoughts and feelings about life. She wants to dream with you about the future. These are not the kinds of things that you can do right before bedtime, hoping that she will be interested in sex. No, these are patterns of life that you need to be sensitive to every day of the week. Make sure that your wife feels connected to you relationally.

"I don't think I can keep up with you." Your sexual appetite can be overwhelming for your wife. Your seemingly insatiable desire might make her feel as though she is not up to the task. This can be a slightly helpless feeling for a woman. When you hear her say things like this, be sensitive and understanding with her. Stop and think about what you have done lately to meet her needs. Be willing to put your desires on hold to give her what she needs. If you are only thinking of yourself, you will make her feel as though she is failing at the only thing that matters to you. Put your wife first in your marriage.

"I am so not thinking about sex right now." Your wife needs for everything to feel in order for her to be in the mood. You may be able to ignore the piles of dirty laundry and dishes soaking in the kitchen sink, but they will very likely bother your wife. Some men are like this when it comes to their workspace. I know I find it difficult to organize my thoughts to complete a complex project when I feel like the room I am working in is a chaotic mess. This is how your wife feels when it comes to sexual intimacy. It's hard for her to relax when there are so many things that don't seem quite right in her house. This is where you come in!

From the moment you get home from work, you can work hard to help create a peaceful, orderly environment for your wife to relax in. If you plop down in front of the TV and let her work circles around you, don't be surprised if she's not in the mood at bedtime. Get up and help her make dinner. After dinner, be the first person up to help clear the table and do the dishes. If you have children, one of the best things that you can do for her is to help them get ready for bed. Getting our four children ready for bed is a herculean task every night. It takes both Stephanie and me to make sure that everything gets done. Help your wife, and she will be more willing to help you!

"I just need to talk through this." Stress kills her sexual desire. Relational difficulties and emotional stress can really hinder your wife's readiness for sex. If she feels burdened by something a person did or said, she's going to feel out of sorts until she works through it. A catty comment from one of her friends or a hard moment with one of the kids can scuttle her interest in sex. An argument with her mother or coworker can ruin her desire for intimacy. Clearly, these kinds of things happen to men as well. The difference is that it so rarely inhibits our desire for sex. In fact, the presence of a stressful situation might even make us feel a stronger need for intimacy. But your wife does not operate this way. She needs an outlet to express all of the things she's troubled with.

One of the best things that you can do for her during times like this is listen. Sit down, get comfortable, and let your wife talk. Make sure that she feels heard. You don't even have to solve her problem if you do a great job listening to her. So often the act of verbalizing what is troubling her will help her sort out her emotions. She needs to talk and you need to listen. Turn off the TV, put the phone down, and listen. Give your wife the gift of your undivided attention. Don't interrupt her and don't correct her. Just listen. She does not need to hear you say, "You are just overreacting," "You are being ridiculous," "If you would've listened to me this never would've happened," or, "This is no big deal; be glad you don't have to deal with real problems like I have at work." If she wants or needs your advice, then render it in the most loving and gentle way possible. Even if you don't have a solution, do your best to encourage her. She needs to hear you say that "Everything is going to be okay." Acknowledge how hard her situation must be for her. You may also want to spend a few moments in prayer together.

"I don't feel very comfortable." Sometimes your wife is not going to feel physically well enough for sex. When you hear her say that she is not feeling comfortable, you need to be sensitive to her needs and forget about your own (at least for the time being). This is your cue to do whatever you can to make her evening much better. Whatever you do, don't make her feel bad for not feeling well enough for intercourse. If she has a headache, rub her head to relax the pain. Go and get her medicine with a glass of water. If her back hurts, rub her back (only her back). If her feet hurt, rub her feet (only her feet). If she is nauseous, maybe you could rub some peppermint oil on her stomach (only her stomach). If she is stressed and exhausted, maybe you could find her favorite book and make her a cup of tea. Don't ignore her discomfort and assume that she will still want to make love to you.

"I am so ready for bed." When she says this, the only nocturnal activity she is thinking about is sleep. I am sorry to disappoint, but it is not secret code for "Let's make passionate love until the wee hours of the morning." When she says, "I am so ready for bed," she never means sex. I know this blows your mind when you think of everything that bedtime could entail. Lovingly understand your wife's exhaustion and let her sleep. She will remember your selflessness. If sexual intimacy is truly about showing love to your wife, then not having sex might be a tangible way to show it on some days. If sex is only about you, then feel free to proceed with whatever selfish, petty response comes most naturally. If sexual intimacy is truly all about producing intimacy, the last thing you want to do is to leverage your sexual frustration to create division in your marriage. How can you demonstrate your love to her while simultaneously making her feel guilty for not making love to you? Try to have a long view. Lead your wife well by showing her what it looks like to lay down your desires. Laying down your preferences to accommodate your wife just may pay huge dividends in the days to come. Your wife will not forget how you valued her feelings above your own. She will recognize that it costs you something dear in order to care for her. If she loves you, she will not let your sacrificial love go unnoticed or unappreciated.

"WHEN HE TOUCHED ME . . . I BRISTLED"

"I still remember where I sat. It was halfway from the front on the left side at the very end of the pew. I was in one of those megachurches, which was a lot different from the Sunday morning crowd where my husband pastored a congregation of 100 people. I had never been to a women's conference like this one, with over a thousand in attendance. But this conference ended up being an answer to prayer.

"A few weeks before this event happened, I was sitting on my couch, crying out to God, 'God, please help me! I do not know what is wrong! I do not understand, and YOU are the ONLY one who can give me an answer!'

"I am married to a wonderful man. We have grown old together and just celebrated over forty years of marriage. Why was I crying out to God? I loved my husband. He is a kind, wonderful man. He is a godly man. He is obviously a patient man. I do not remember when it began, but when he touched me, I just bristled. I did not want to be touched. Intimacy was out of the question. I do not know what happened or why it happened.

"My supervisor at work had registered to attend the 'Women's Conference.' She had a conflict in her schedule and asked me if I wanted to go. She knew nothing about what was going on in my life. I jumped at the chance, not really looking for the answer, but probably looking for an excuse to get away.

"One of the seminars was on 'Sexual Intimacy in Marriage.' A required seminar for first-time guests. The speaker was amazing. Her spirit shined. She was funny and entertaining and serious all at the same time. One of the main topics in this seminar was 'Frigidity in Marriage'! There it was—my problem. Now I needed God's answer!

"I come from 'dysfunctional family' roots. I did not have the happy family with a loving mom and dad. My grandparents raised me, which was such a blessing. I am so thankful they were willing to do that! I do not have one good memory of my earthly father. He was a mean man. My times with him as a child were riddled with fear and confusion. I am sure my mother was in the picture somewhere, and I can say this about my mom: I do feel like she loved me; though, at the same time, I felt abandoned by her. With good ole Dad, I NEVER felt loved, protected, or anything positive from him. However, they were both alcoholics, so my visits with them were never enjoyable. I usually had to be the adult in their drunken world, regardless of my age.

"The incredible speaker at the women's conference started talking about forgiveness. She quoted Bible verses and made her case for the importance of dismissing hurt, wrongs, injustice, and giving them all to God. She explained how harboring the feelings and pain from the past does not hurt the offender, but it hurts me . . . the offended! Then she explained the importance and urgency of *forgiving* that one individual or group that has caused the hurt and pain!

"All those times that my dad hurt me . . . emotionally abused me . . . was cruel to me . . . I had to forgive him? Really, God?! I argued with God for what seemed a long time, but the matter was settled by the time the invitation ended. In my distress and anguish, I surrendered this much, saying: 'God, I can't do this. But I know you can do this through me . . . so I give it all to you—all the pain, the disappointment, and the injury from my father. I will forgive him, but I can only do so with your help.'

"Peace, relief, and a lifted burden are what I felt. I still had a lot to learn about this forgiveness thing. Like you must keep doing it—over and over—every time you harbor those ill feelings. I have forgiven my 'dad' on many occasions though the years. My dad had passed away, so my forgiveness goes through God. There are occasions when it is necessary to tell the abuser about your forgiveness toward them. I also had to learn to forgive every time I was offended or hurt by anyone. When I felt resentment, anger, or bitterness, I knew it was time to evaluate the situation and go to God with it.

"Forgiveness is not an easy thing. We like to say things such as, 'You do not know what they/he/she did to me!' or, 'How can anyone forgive that?' or, 'You would not forgive them either!' But forgiveness is for the offended, not the offender. It benefits the one hurting, not the one causing the hurt. Bear with each other and forgive each other if you have a grievance against someone. 'Forgive as the Lord forgave you' (Col. 3:13). 'For if you forgive other people when they sin against you, your heavenly Father will also forgive you. But if you do not forgive others their sins, your father will not forgive your sins' (Matt. 6:14–15). 'Get rid of all bitterness, rage and anger, brawling and slander, along with every form of malice. Be kind and compassionate one to another, forgiving each other, just as in Christ, God forgave you' (Eph. 4:31–32).

"Contribute to your peace and happiness through forgiveness. God will bless you and your marriage abundantly as you obey His Word."

—Married 45 Years

Admittedly, sex in marriage may not always seem like a feast. But by submitting yourself to the Lord, He can give you the grace to minister to your spouse in the ways that they need the most. Sometimes this will lead to sex, and other times He may prompt you to lay down your desire because your spouse has a more pressing need. A wonderful feast is oftentimes accompanied by a deep sense of satisfaction.

Satisfaction. Feasting should lead to a glorious satisfaction. There is nothing like having a belly full of your favorite foods. After a great feast, all you want to do is relax and think about how wonderful the meal was. "Where did you get that recipe?" "The mashed potatoes were incredible!" "Let's eat that same chocolate roll every Christmas Eve!" After an amazing meal, you can't help but continue to think about it. Isn't it nice to see contentment on the faces of those we love? Sometimes, though, a wonderful feast turns into a wonderful nap, and that's okay too! And if the food was really amazing, you will be headed back to the fridge before long to heat up the leftovers! But the satisfaction of a great meal pales in comparison to the fulfillment that sexual intimacy can create within a godly marriage.

Feasting in marriage should lead to the kind of satisfaction that nothing else in life can. As you tenderly care for the needs of your spouse, God creates a wonderful gratification that will leave you returning to the table over and over again. Nobody else in the world can satisfy your spouse in this manner. You are the only one who can bring this kind of fulfillment into your marriage. Strive to understand the needs of your spouse. Then love your spouse enough to spread a banquet for them. Give of yourself to the point where your spouse can't take another bite. Work to make sure that both of you receive the sexual diet that God intends for you to have. Then watch with amazement how God uses this nourishment to strengthen your marriage. It is never too late to recapture the joy of feasting in your marriage!

"SEXUALLY AVAILABLE"

"I don't always want to make love to my husband. I believe that it's okay to have those feelings. I feel so thankful that my husband has been tender toward me and tries not to make me feel guilty when those moments happen. But I think one of the primary reasons he is patient and gentle with me is because he knows and trusts that I will love him and take care of his needs. I think we both respect not just the needs that we have but also the wants and desires of the other person.

"The Lord has impressed upon me the importance of loving my

husband well, especially in regard to the marriage bed. I often pray for the Lord's protection on my marriage and that the Lord would grow my love for my husband. I love my husband very much, but I strongly believe my marriage needs the tender care of the Lord's hands. There are times when my husband's sexual needs feel overwhelming to me because it is sometimes a daily physical need. Because of who I am and how I am wired, my response to life is not usually 'Let's go have sex.'

"But his is.

"I think the common response is to undervalue what sex means to him because I don't understand it most of the time. I do not want my husband degrading and ignoring the significance of what makes me feel loved, so why would I want to do that to him?

"There are many ways in which I am selfish, and I fail at times, but I do feel that the Lord has given me a special tenderness in this one area of intimacy. Being available to my husband and showing him love when I don't feel up to it is a way I can show selfless love to him. I also trust that my husband will show me selfless love in the ways that I need it. My needs can be very different from his, but he is always quick to want to provide those for me.

"God has used Proverbs 31:11, 'Her husband has full confidence in her and lacks nothing of value' in my life. I desire that my husband will trust me with this intimate issue. Just because his need is different from mine does not mean that it is of less importance. As I pray for my husband, God allows me to be more tender and sexually available to him. God gives me the strength to be selfless in an intimate way."

—Married 11 Years

Homework

1. When was the last time sex felt like a banquet? What was it that made the experience so wonderful?
2. Complete the following sentence: "When I start feeling hungry for intimacy, I have a tendency to . . ."

3. Complete the following sentence: "Sex leaves me feeling full when we . . ."
4. When it comes to providing a feast, discuss some things you tend to struggle with.
5. Think of ways to make your bedroom more of a banquet hall, then execute your plan and provide a feast.
6. Think of one way to communicate love to your spouse this week, and implement it.

A Prayer for You

"Father, every good and perfect gift comes from you, oh Lord. You give generously to all. Thank you for allowing us the opportunity to both give and receive the gift of sexual intimacy. Help us to provide a rich bounty for each other. Teach us the joy of giving sacrificially to each other in this special way. Help us not to take each other for granted. Grant us your grace to treat each other with the utmost care and sensitivity. Guard our hearts from the kind of selfishness that might hinder our sexual intimacy. Give us the strength, time, and energy to devote to providing a banquet for each other. Help us never grow weary when it comes to nourishing each other in this special way.

"As we seek you with all of our hearts, help us to develop a healthy and mutually satisfying banquet for each other. Help us to establish a healthy rhythm for sexual intimacy in our marriage. Kindle a deep and abiding passion for each other. Help us to cultivate a greater appetite for only each other. Guard us from the sin of feasting our eyes on any other person. Help us not to interact with each other in petty ways that would hinder the kind of banquet spoken about in the Song of Solomon. Help us to savor each other and to enjoy a long lifetime of wonderful intimacy! In Jesus' name, Amen."

CLOSING THOUGHTS

You get to decide in your own marriage how you want to finish the phrase, "Sex is. . . ." Every couple will finish this phrase differently in their marriage. Here are some of the options to choose from. You can finish the phrase in really positive ways, such as, "Sex is the fabulous expression of the wonderful love that we have for each other," or, "Sex is the awesome gift of God that we take full advantage of." There are also some very sad ways to finish off the phrase "Sex is. . . ." Some might say, "Sex is the thing that we fight most about in our marriage." Still others might say, "Sex is completely uninteresting in our marriage." How will you and your spouse finish the phrase?

God has given you such a wonderful gift, and He wants you to experience the best of it in your marriage. He intends for the pleasure of sexual intimacy to drive you toward your spouse in a passionate pursuit that never ends. A godly marriage is the ideal paradigm for you to enjoy the best of what God intended for sexual intimacy to be. Sexual intimacy will flourish as you cultivate a stronger love and a deeper friendship with your spouse. You will reap a bountiful harvest as you learn to admire and treasure your spouse for who God made them to be. Remember, as important as the joy of your marriage is, there is far more at stake. And the ultimate purpose behind sexual intimacy is not really about *you*!

That's why it really matters how you finish the phrase "Sex is. . . ." Wonderful intimacy promotes strong marriages that impact the world for Christ! God blessed you with a spouse who will help you maximize your impact for the Lord Jesus Christ. How can you serve effectively in your church if you are unhappy in your marriage? How can you show a lost world the love of Christ if your marriage is languishing in turmoil? Why would lost people want anything to do with your God if they see you so unhappy in your marriage? How can we share the love of Christ with strangers in the world if we cannot even show it to our spouse? Sexual intimacy is such an important component of strong marriages. So important, in fact, that when it is purposefully neglected, it can cause tremendous problems. Strong marriages cultivate stronger churches.

Serving the Lord and sharing the love of Jesus Christ is very difficult. So many challenges await those who are truly passionate about piercing the darkness of this world with the good news of the gospel. Only those marriages that are rock solid will have a tremendous impact for the Lord in our world. Strong marriages fortify and make you resilient in your service to the Lord. What a blessing it is to have your best friend and lover beside you every step of the way as you shine the light of Jesus Christ. In every moment where you might be tempted to call it quits, you will have your greatest friend cheering you on and encouraging you toward faithfulness. When doubts and frustration mount, you can pray for each other to remain strong in the Lord. Make sexual intimacy a priority in your marriage and watch God strengthen your relationship with your spouse. God will leverage the strength of your marriage so that others can know Jesus Christ!

A COVENANT FOR YOU

I am so proud of you for completing this journey through Song of Solomon with your spouse. You have prayed together about sexual intimacy. You have studied what God's Word has to say about it. You have openly discussed the principles explained in this book and have learned so much about each other. But your marriage will not improve unless you do the things that you have learned. Only you can turn this understanding into action. I now invite you to express to each other your earnest commitment to love each other excellently by signing the covenant below.

* * *

By God's grace and by the power of the Holy Spirit I will strive in the following areas:

I will not take you for granted.

I will live with gratitude toward God for giving me this wonderful gift of sexual intimacy.

I will strive to live out my love for the Lord Jesus Christ by loving you intimately.

I will do my best to treat your needs as more important than mine.

I will be willing to inconvenience myself in order to love you better.

I will labor to affirm you by expressing my admiration and adoration for you.

I will do a better job in verbalizing the things that are going on in my heart.

I will try to become a better listener.

I will pray regularly for God to unify us so that we might serve Christ more effectively together.

I will seek Christ through His Word and prayer so that I might refresh you.

I will try to spend more time with you, devoting time and energy to being your best friend.

I will say "no" to every form of sexual temptation.

I will be a locked garden to the world, but a vineyard of pleasure and delight for you.

I will put more time and effort into providing a banquet for you.

I will never stop pursuing you.

If you are willing to strive in these areas, please sign on the lines below.

Husband: X____________________ Date: _________

Wife: X____________________ Date: _________

Appendix 1

MANAGING DISPROPORTIONATE SEXUAL DESIRES

In the best of marriages, there will be seasons where there is a disproportionate desire when it comes to sex. In fact, this is a normal challenge in most marriages. Even when you are faithfully doing many of the things talked about in this book, there may be times when you don't feel like your spouse shares your same need for sex. In most cases, it will be the husband who feels like he's not getting enough sex. But this is not always the case in every marriage. Some wives will find themselves very troubled at their husband's lack of sexual desire. Every marriage is different and deals with a unique set of challenges. What should you do if you find yourself in this kind of disproportionate experience?

If your marriage is experiencing a long drought caused by factors outside of your control, it may be best to sit down with a Christian counselor. However, many couples will be able to navigate through their disproportionate desire. Below are a few suggestions that you can put to work right away. The lists below are by no means exhaustive, but they hopefully will serve as a starting place for you in your marriage.

If Your Spouse Doesn't Want Sex

1. **Pray for your spouse**. God formed the heart of every living thing. If you trust in Christ, believe that He is able to give your spouse a greater desire for you. Better yet, pray for your spouse to have an insatiable appetite for you. Ask God to help you to become the person that your spouse will desire. Pray for God to alleviate the stress and pressure that they are under. Pray that God would give your spouse more energy for sex. Pray for your spouse to understand your physical needs. Pray for God to orchestrate your spouse's day so that they have time for you sexually. You should also spend time thanking God for your spouse. Even if you are frustrated at the moment, you have so much to be thankful for. God answers prayer.

2. **Give grace**. News flash—your spouse is not perfect! Every person goes through seasons in life. Give your spouse time. One of the beautiful things about marriage is that there is always plenty of time. In a godly marriage, time is your friend, not your enemy. Keep pursuing your spouse intimately and in every other way. Often their interest in sex will rebound as quickly as it seemed to dissipate. During this time, do your best to try to understand what your spouse might be going through.

3. **Resist the urge to become bitter**. Aside from being incredibly unattractive, bitterness is a great way to diminish your sex life. Remember: "Love is patient, love is kind" (1 Cor. 13:4). If you want your spouse to be patient with you in your weaknesses, you must be patient with them in theirs. Labor to forgive and love your spouse even when their sexual desire for you is not what you want it to be.

4. **Work hard at becoming the person God has called you to be**. It would be much easier to sit around thinking of all the ways your spouse is not what you want them to be. But what about you? Are you growing in your relationship with the Lord Jesus? Are you striving to be all that your spouse needs you to be?

Spend time with the Lord cultivating the kind of godly heart that will draw your spouse closer to you. You cannot control what your spouse does or doesn't do, but you can control what you do. You need to work on the part that you can change and stop being consumed with the things that you can't change.

5. **Don't use guilt**. The last thing you want to do is use guilt to manipulate your spouse into the bedroom. Don't pout or feel sorry for yourself when your spouse has disappointed you. Don't give your spouse the cold shoulder or silent treatment. Don't make your spouse feel there is something wrong with them when they are not in the mood. Even if you succeed in satisfying your immediate need, it does nothing to help you in the long run. Do your best to see the big picture. Have a long view of your temporary disappointment. Your sex life will not flourish if you cultivate an environment where you make your spouse feel bad about themselves for not desiring you sexually.
6. **Be understanding**. If you know that your wife is six months pregnant, you need to be more understanding. Don't expect your sex life to remain unchanged when your wife is uncomfortable. By the same token, if your husband is temporarily on the night shift, be understanding with his fatigue. As you go through difficult seasons in life, be reasonable about your expectations of your spouse.
7. **Don't give up**. God made you to express your sexuality with your spouse. Don't give up on this part of your marriage if you are having a difficult time. Talk through the issue with your spouse. Read a Christian book on intimacy. Work on it and pray through it, but do not give up. Sexual intimacy is too important for you to give up on.
8. **Don't take your needs elsewhere**. Your spouse's lack of libido does not give you a license to take your sexual needs elsewhere. Those who take on a victim mentality might be tempted to rationalize sexual sin. Shame, grief, regret, pain, and remorse

await those who sin sexually. The only godly sexual expression is between you and your spouse. Every deviation from this mold is sinful.

9. **Defer to the needs of your spouse**. Intimacy is one of many areas where you will need to learn to accommodate the needs of your spouse. Those needs may change over time, but the constant should be your earnest desire to sacrificially love your spouse. You need to accept that there will be many occasions where you will need to give your spouse what they need instead of what you desire. If they need to relax instead of make love, then help them relax. If your spouse needs to talk, let them talk. If it's time alone that they need, give them time. But if your spouse never seems to be in the mood, then deferring to the needs of your spouse may not be a long-term strategy.
10. **Make the next time unforgettable**. The moment is coming when the twinkle will return to your spouse's eye. When it does, do your best to make sure that they never forget just how wonderful sex is. Lavish them with the kind of care and attention that you yourself crave. Give your spouse the beautiful memory of a wonderful sexual experience with you, and they will very likely come back for more!

If You Don't Want Sex

1. **Do unto others**. What if the shoe was on the other foot? What if you felt as though your spouse did not desire you? How would this make you feel? If the roles were reversed, how would you want your spouse to treat you? Do the very best you can to love your spouse intimately even when you are not in the mood. So often, when it comes to obedience, feelings follow actions. You may find that your desire will follow your actions.
2. **Say, "I'm sorry."** Apologizing is one of the best ways to acknowledge the hurt that you have caused your spouse. If you don't apologize, your spouse might feel like you don't even

care about how much they feel rejected. A good old-fashioned "I'm sorry" can go a long way to reestablishing positive lines of communication.

3. **Be honest**. Sometimes you cannot help the way you feel. If stress, sleepless nights, or a baby with colic has rendered you without any desire for sex, talk to your spouse. Do not allow your spouse to imagine what's going on with you. Explain it to your spouse so that they know what's going on. Don't leave them in the dark. It's not in your best interest for them to start thinking that they are no longer attractive to you or that you don't even love them anymore. You cannot expect your spouse to be understanding if you have not communicated what's going on with you. Even if you don't know what's going on, you still need to have the conversation so you can try to figure it out as a couple.
4. **Find the problem**. Not wanting to make love to your spouse may not be the problem; rather, it could be a symptom of a problem. Do your best to work through what's going on in your life. Ask the Lord to show you why you find it so difficult to make love to your spouse. Do you have some imbalance in your life? Are you getting enough rest? What are you doing for fun? Ask yourself what would make you desire your spouse more. Is there something in your past that's making things difficult? Are you angry about something? Is there somebody that you need to forgive? There may also be a medical problem keeping you from desiring sexual intimacy. Maybe it's time to make an appointment with your doctor. It could be that there is a very simple solution to your lack of sexual drive. For the sake of your marriage, get to the bottom of the problem.
5. **Live well**. Your desire for your spouse will grow as you pursue a healthy life. Exercise, eat well, and take good care of yourself. A deficiency in any of these areas could make matters much worse. Part of living well is resting. If you are not sleeping

enough and are overworked, it's no wonder that you don't feel in the mood. Discipline yourself to get good rest each night. If work has become all consuming, do your best to create healthy boundaries. Ask God to help you live with a healthy balance. Remember, you may have many jobs over the course of your career, but a spouse is for life!

6. **Something is much better than nothing**. If you don't feel capable of providing your spouse with a rich sexual experience, maybe there is something that you can do to meet the need. When it comes to satisfying your spouse sexually, something will always be better than nothing. What can you do to minister to your spouse even though you don't feel capable of making love?
7. **Spend more time together**. Spending time with your lover will help you want to make love to them. Sit with your spouse and talk about your hopes and dreams. Turn off the television and share a cup of coffee on the back porch. Take the earbuds out, set the screens down, and talk to your lover. Take a walk in the cool of the evening, holding hands. Play a game that both of you enjoy. A little playful banter and healthy competition will help you focus on each other. Sip your favorite iced tea and share your favorite memories of each other. Plan an unforgettable date with your spouse. Buy the tickets, make the reservations, book the hotel. Go for it. Your marriage is worth the time, the effort, and the money. Making a special memory together will only help your love life. Get a babysitter and go to your favorite restaurant.
8. **Think about intimacy with your spouse**. It's hard to be in the mood when you have not been in the mood for a while. If you don't think about sex with your spouse, there's a good chance that you will not want to have sex with your spouse. Actions so often follow our thoughts. You may need to energize yourself by intentionally thinking about your spouse in that special way.

It is a healthy and helpful thing to think sexually about your spouse. Think back to all of those wonderful moments that you shared together. Remember all of the things that attracted you to your spouse in the first place. Think about the next sexual moment that you might share together.

9. **Pray**. If God designed sex to be a unifying thing in your marriage, then you can and should pray about sex. Ask God to give you a stronger desire to make love to your spouse. Ask the Lord to help you take great care of your spouse sexually. Ask the Lord to bring about a renewed season of joy in your bedroom. Ask Him to identify areas of your life that need to change so you can experience the best of what He intended sex to be in your marriage. Ask the Lord to show you how to be a great lover for your spouse.
10. **Defer to the needs of your spouse**. If you are able, try to defer to the needs of your spouse. The needs of your spouse are just as important as your needs. Try hard not to minimize your spouse's needs by ignoring their sexual needs. Sacrificially loving your spouse is always a good thing. Notice I included this on both lists. By challenging both of you to defer to each other's needs, perhaps one of you will have the grace to minister to the other when it seems hard. So long as one of you has the grace to do the selfless thing, you'll likely avert a crisis. If, however, both of you persist and stand your selfish ground, strife will be the unavoidable conclusion.

Bibliography

Barna Group. "What Americans Believe about Sex," January 14, 2016. https://www.barna.com/research/what-americans-believe-about-sex/.

Cave, James. "This Abandoned Pennsylvania Town Has Been on Fire for 53 Years." *Huffington Post,* January 9, 2017. http://www.huffingtonpost.com/entry/this-abandoned-pennsylvania-town-has-been-on-fire-for-53-years_us_55df6490e4b08dc09486d4a0.

Chapell, Bryan. *Each for the Other.* Grand Rapids: Baker Books, 2005.

Chapman, Gary. *Now What: The Chapman Guide to Marriage after Children.* Carol Stream, IL: Tyndale, 2009.

———. *The Five Love Languages: How to Express Heartfelt Commitment to Your Mate.* Chicago: Northfield Publishing, 2004.

———. *The 4 Seasons of Marriage: Secrets to a Lasting Marriage.* Wheaton, IL: Tyndale House, 2012.

Farrel, Bill and Pam Farrel. *Red-Hot Monogamy.* Eugene, OR: Harvest House, 2006.

Fee, Gordon D. *The First Epistle to the Corinthians.* The New International Commentary on the New Testament. Grand Rapids: Wm. B. Eerdmans, 1987.

Garrett, Duane A. *Proverbs, Ecclesiastes, Song of Songs.* New American Commentary. Nashville: Broadman, 1993.

Garrett, Duane A. and Paul R. House. *Song of Songs/Lamentations.* Word Biblical Commentary, Book 23. Nashville: Thomas Nelson, 2004.

Isom, Mo. *Sex, Jesus and the Conversations the Church Forgot.* Grand Rapids: Baker Books, 2018.

Keller, Timothy. *The Meaning of Marriage: Facing the Complexities of Commitment with the Wisdom of God.* New York: Riverhead Books, 2011.

Kinnaman, David. "The Porn Phenomenon." Barna Group, February 5, 2016. https://www.barna.com/the-porn-phenomenon/.

Leman, Kevin. *Sheet Music: Uncovering the Secrets of Sexual Intimacy in Marriage.* Carol Stream, IL: Tyndale, 2008.

Parrott, Les and Leslie Parrott. *I Love You More.* Grand Rapids: Zondervan, 2005.

Pew Research Center. "The Decline of Marriage and the Rise of New Families." November 18, 2010. http://www.pewsocialtrends.org/2010/11/18/ii-overview/.

Smalley, Gary and John Trent. *The Language of Love: A Powerful Way to Maximize Insight, Intimacy, and Understanding.* Pomona, CA: Focus on the Family Publishing, 1988.

Stuart, Douglas. *Exodus: An Exegetical and Theological Exposition of Holy Scripture.* The New American Commentary. Nashville: Broadman and Holman, 2006.

Thomas, Gary. *Cherish: The One Word That Changes Everything for Your Marriage.* Grand Rapids: Zondervan, 2017.

———. *Sacred Marriage: What If God Designed Marriage to Make Us Holy More Than to Make Us Happy?* Grand Rapids: Zondervan, 2000.

Tripp, Paul David. *Sex in a Broken World: How Christ Redeems What Sin Distorts. Wheaton,* IL: Crossway, 2018.

Other Books by Kevin J. Moore

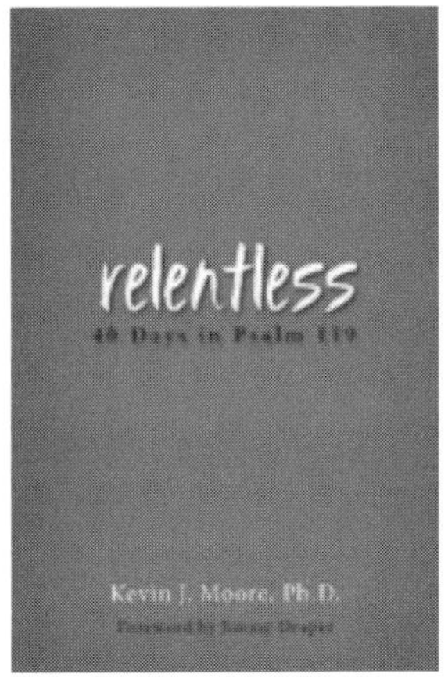

Relentless will guide you on an unforgettable 40-day journey through the longest Psalm of the Bible, Psalm 119. Every morning devotional and evening prayer presents a concise and Christ-centered focus that will challenge you to pursue a more committed relationship with Jesus. *Relentless* will lead your small group or congregation to develop an insatiable appetite for God's Word that will translate into reaching a lost world. This inspiring and provocative exploration of Psalm 119 will open your eyes to the inestimable beauty of God's Word and ignite within you a relentless desire for more of Him. You will never be the same!

Built around seven powerful expressions of love, *Holy Rebellion* draws lessons from real-life ministry encounters. Wedged tightly into each story is the most powerful lesson a pastor could ever learn—the message of love. From cover to cover, *Holy Rebellion* takes you on a vivid journey through the most glorious victories and embarrassing blunders in pastoral ministry. From being compared to a primate and proof of Darwin's theory of evolution to falsely congratulating a woman on her pregnancy, you'll come face-to-face with both the awkward and hilarious moments in ministry. This book also explores the imperfection of pastors who at times fail miserably. Books that gloss over the painful times in ministry that were self-induced do little to edify pastors who struggle with the consequences of their mistakes. *Holy Rebellion* is fresh, honest, and compelling.

Connect With Kevin...

Kevin would love to hear how the Lord used this book to strengthen your marriage. If you would like to share your story, here's how you can connect with him…

Website: www.kevinjmoore.me

Email: authorkevinjmoore@gmail.com

Facebook: Facebook.com/authorkevinmoore